Keep Yo
Beth !,

The Miseducation of Empathy

Jonelle Massey (signature)

JONELLE MASSEY

psychotherapist

The Miseducation of Empathy

Copyright © 2021 by Jonelle Massey

For permission requests or to contact the author, visit: jonellemassey.com

ISBN-13: 978-1-7365220-0-4

Printed in the United States of America

THE MISEDUCATION OF EMPATHY

Jonelle Massey

psychotherapist

*For my dad's reliability, simplicity,
and ease that comforts me.*

*For my mom's resilience and
tireless love that inspires me.*

*For my husband's heart and
protection that follows me.*

*For my oldest girl's faith, ambition,
and kindness that empowers me.*

*For my baby girl's affectionate yet
sedulous spirit that strengthens me.*

For my grandmother's legacy that assures me.

For them, I dedicate this...

CONTENTS

Keep Yourself in Your Own Shoes..i

Empathy is Not Sacrifice...1
A Coach's Wife's Journey Toward Empathy

Empathy is Not Sympathy..19
Your Sorry Makes Me Feel Sorry

Empathy is Not Vicarious Feelings...............................35
College and the Search for Connection

Empathy is Not Innate...59
What the Streets of Bond Hill Taught Me

The Reeducation of Empathy...75
Relearning Our ABCs

Acknowledging Humanity...77
If the Shoe Fits, Wear It: Fear of Association

Bypass Your Feelings to Validate Theirs................91
Tipping the Scale: Comparison is the Thief of Empathy

Connect Beliefs...109
There is Safety in Your Thoughts: The Games We Play

Archetypes of Empathy...119

The Cheerleader
The Blanket
The Operator
The Fixer-Upper
The Crossing Guard

Empathy's Reputation is on the Line.....................................155

About the Author

Keep Yourself in Your Own Shoes

Empathy. The trendiest three-syllable, seven letter word that changed my life and has the reputation for changing the world. We see it on posters in school hallways, in office training manuals, printed as topics in leadership conference programs, preached in sermons at the pulpit of churches, passionately shouted about in political speeches, mentioned on thousands of TED talk stages, and strategically placed in bold font on countless social media memes. I've come to expect empathy to be a part of most self-growth conversations, because mainstream culture collectively agrees that empathy is the starting point for solving both small and complex social problems—it is the activating agent for connection. *How do we battle racism and discrimination?* The foundation must start with empathy. *How can teachers leave a bigger impact on their students?* They must be more empathetic to students' needs. *How do we create a better work culture?* Empathy. *How can we be a better friend, ally, and spouse? How should we live and work with difficult people? How can we live in a more peaceful union?* Empathy. Empathy. Empathy.

If it is common knowledge that empathy is essential in solving so many problems, why don't we appear to be a more empathetic nation? If what I so desperately needed as a child, young adult, married woman, and mother was empathy, why was I so confused and misled by it?

I'll tell you why. My life experiences taught me that our traditional concept of empathy doesn't provide us with a foundational understanding and framework of the relationship between thoughts and feelings, which must be the basis for empathy. I can't walk in your shoes and you can't walk in mine. I can't feel what you're feeling, and I can't understand the feelings you're experiencing without first understanding the thoughts behind them. Our concept of empathy is misleading, self-serving, and outdated. It doesn't require us to deeply invest in others, rather only to imagine how they must feel. If empathy doesn't require a deep and personal investment of understanding beyond vicarious feelings, how can we ever expect it to produce a meaningful and personal impact? Human beings need connection to feel understood, yet we have been looking at it all wrong – walking it out from the wrong pair of shoes.

We have been taught that empathy is this vague construct of relating. It has been defined as the near impossible task to feel what others are feeling. And we have the audacity to begin asking this of people when they're as young as five years old. School-aged children are expected and taught to empathize by dissociating or disconnecting from their own emotions in order to identify with their peers'. This is a nearly insurmountable task for most adults, let alone our children. Empathy has to be more attainable than trying to teleport yourself into someone else's perspective, expectations, feelings... shoes.

As a mom, wife, psychotherapist, and school counselor, I recognize the wealth and power empathy holds, and whenever I fail at being empathetic it's usually because I have reverted back to this confusing and frustrating traditional model of empathy. I try to remove myself – my own experiences, thoughts, and feelings – from the equation so I can then put myself in someone else's shoes. It's easy to slip back into this traditional formula of empathy because it's ingrained in us to identify it this way. I slip up and try on my husband's shoes and fail. Take off my shoes and try to squeeze into my best friend's shoes and fail. I've endured years of frustration trying to teach my students to put themselves in someone else's shoes until I finally realized that empathy can't exist unless both parties keep their own shoes on.

Shoes are meant to fit one pair of feet at one time, because our experiences are singular and subjective, and we should respect this about ourselves. A deep and mutual connection can only come through two individual people sharing. Being able to connect to the same thought - recognizing that the same thought may come from differing experiences and differing feelings - adds layered meaning to a connection. My husband and I both had the same thought our first couple of years of marriage: "I want more." This thought manifested different feelings between my husband and I, and this thought was based on two totally different experiences as husband and wife. Identifying and understanding shared thoughts is deeper than trying to replicate a person's feelings, and leads to more intimate growth and a more loving marriage.

Most of my time as a therapist is spent helping my clients discover, process and reframe, if needed, their interpretation or thoughts about things that happen to them - especially events out of their control. This process of examining thoughts can potentially open the door to changing how my clients feel. Human beings have the power to change and choose how they feel through the interpretations of what's happening, although it may feel like an impossible superpower at times. But we all possess this superpower. It is the superpower that helps us feel better about a decision that we regret. It is the superpower that motivates us to keep applying and interviewing for the next job. It is the superpower that pushes our feelings of immense guilt towards feelings of acceptance through the reframing of our thoughts. But I have to be honest. Examining our thoughts and the thoughts of others is intentional hard work that doesn't always come easy. It makes sense that it is hard work. No reward as great as empathy could come so easily. And that's why we need a framework to guide us through.

Miseducation of empathy has proven very frustrating to practice because it requires an osmosis of feelings with vague skills to "just do it." We tell people to imagine what someone else might be feeling, but we aren't taught exactly how to do that. Yet we are deemed insensitive or heartless when it doesn't come natural to "just do it." It's careless to think we each have a natural ability to understand another person's emotions when much of the time we don't understand our own. Emotions are complicated, layered, subjective, and don't always make sense, not to mention each of us have varying intensities of similar emotions. When we reduce the meaning of empathy to a simple metaphor, the essence and impact of empathy falls short. Our current perspective of empathy doesn't set the clear groundwork for change and doesn't have any significant, long-term impact on solving problems. It's simply not living up to its reputation.

The traditional concept of empathy is also confusing and frustrating because it recognizes the importance of understanding other people's feelings but, at the same time, suggests that we then include our own emotions in the mix - stepping into their shoes.

Emotions are keys that unlock what is inside; the passwords that allow us to enter into the database of a person's thoughts, which is why they deserve to be acknowledged and validated. When we feel like someone important to us doesn't understand us, it's because we think they don't or can't understand how we feel. We don't actually need other people to feel exactly what we feel. In fact, we are typically frustrated that it is impossible for them to ever feel what we are feeling. What's missing is our desire to be understood, how we think about a thing. We need other people to understand the thought processes behind our feelings – so we can feel in solidarity and justified in the feelings these thoughts conjure.

When we make space for a person to feel their emotions, when they feel permission to express exactly how they feel, we stop short if we don't then encourage further investigation. An investigation of our thoughts helps validate both our feelings and our humanity. Thoughts are the starting point and not the finish line to making connections of understanding with others. When I focus my parenting on uncovering the wants and perspectives of my children, I become better connected and able to share in understanding of both their motivations and feelings.

Our lack of shared mutual understanding perpetuates our diminishing faith in connection, a shared oneness, compromise, and human decency. Because of the miseducation of empathy, we are moving further and further away from human, even though we think we are being noble in our fraught pursuit to try and encourage empathy. Our current beliefs about empathy is a breeding ground for conflict and resentment. I must take my shoes off in order to put yours on, which implies I must remove my perspective, my experiences, my feelings, thoughts, and thus my personal opportunity to try and authentically understand yours. This type of traditional empathy also makes for bad marital advice.

The current definition of empathy implies we must make a sacrifice to properly practice empathy. It asks that someone first give something up (take my shoes off) in order to understand and be empathetic (put their shoes on). By sacrificing our own perspective and understanding, we don't leave any room for connection, we can't build a bridge of shared understanding between two people. In this way, essentially, we have been taught that the practice of empathy is a monologue between two people. You are to imagine others' feelings regardless whether or not you know what it feels like to

be a man
be pregnant

experience racism
struggle with addiction
have the pressure to provide for a family
lose a parent
have that kind of faith
grow up poor
receive a diagnosis
be a college coach's wife

We teach people who have been vulnerable enough to tell and share their truth of not feeling what others are feeling, to ignore it, and ignore who they are, in an attempt to walk in the truth of another. Just do it. But there is still room for empathy right in the middle of YOUR truth, even if it doesn't feel like theirs. Personally, I've never felt suicidal, but I can remember thinking things like,

I can't do anything to change my situation.
I don't have the help that I need.
This is not how I envisioned my life.
I want to run away from everything.

In order to find connected thoughts under layers of emotions and spoken words, we have to actively listen from inside our own shoes. Through active intentional listening and validation, you can show empathy and connected understanding about a situation that you've never experienced through a more balanced connection. And this is possible not only when it comes to situations you've never experienced but also with people you don't know or don't like.

Real empathy crosses all boundaries – gender, race, religion, politics. And real empathy even opens up the door for you to be empathetic with yourself. The miseducation of empathy would define self-empathy as understanding your feelings by putting yourself in your own shoes. What does that even mean and how is this helpful? Real empathy opens the door for me to validate my feelings, investigate, and connect with and understand my own thoughts. Real empathy saved my marriage. Real empathy, not other people's attempts at feeling what I am feeling, dug me out of unbearable guilt. People sharing in my sorrow didn't carry me over feelings of loneliness and isolation, but genuine empathy did. In my pursuit to feel deeper and more healing connections to other people, I have uncovered the essence of true empathy, and it continues to impact the decisions I make, the friends I keep, and the interactions I choose and value. It supports my confidence and guides my purpose. It provides meaningful relationships that keep my family and sustain my hope for a better future. And most importantly, it validates all of who I am and who God calls me to be. Empathy provokes love, compassion, patience, effective communication, conflict resolution, and forgiveness. It's about time we set the record straight about the miseducation of empathy because

my marriage
your friends
our children
your coworkers
my schools
our communities
your ministries
our government
humanity

can no longer afford to be misled by unrealistic metaphors, vague notions, and hopeful attempts at teleported feelings.

CHAPTER ONE

Empathy is Not Sacrifice

A Coach's Wife's Journey Toward Empathy

On August 6th, 2005, my on-again, off-again boyfriend sat across from me on my brown loveseat and interrupted me with a request for something to drink. He interrupted our very serious, tense conversation about commitment, purpose, finances, and his future career in coaching as an assistant basketball coach at Robert Morris University. Although I'm annoyed by his beverage request, I stand up, walk around the corner to my small galley kitchen, look in my half-empty refrigerator, and yell out, "Is orange Kool-Aid okay?"

Still visibly bothered by the interruption of our important conversation, I speed walk back to the living room, remembering where I left off and all that I want to reiterate. I turn the corner to find my boyfriend on one knee with a ring in his hand. "Will you marry me?" he asks quickly.

I pause.

"Do you still want this orange Kool-Aid?" I ask.

His proposal is not what I'd imagined it would be, and neither is my response.

Over the last year, I had become more and more impatient with our relationship. Jeff Massey was not sticking to the plan. I had a detailed outline of "next steps." He would retire from playing basketball overseas, take twelve to sixteen months to grieve not playing anymore, then we would get married and start a family. Jeff could figure out his career along the way. Financially, emotionally, and physically, this plan worked - at least that's the way I saw it. My biological clock was ticking as I approached twenty-eight, and we were financially in a position to think about family first. Choosing me before choosing a career made perfect sense to me. I expected it would all just go this way, which becomes a theme in my life.

Jeff is not totally surprised by my Kool-Aid answer. He knows the timing was awkward as we had not been on good terms. He patiently waits back at his place while I decompress the question and my thoughts around it. I ask that he give me some space to think it through. I think and pray overnight by myself, on my brown couch. I don't sleep well, and although I want to talk to all of the wise women in my circle, I know it's best to just sit in my home with my prayers and my thoughts. I think about how Jeff followed his own plan, waiting to start his coaching career before making a marital commitment. I pray about my bitterness toward his noncompliance with the plan I think better suits us, and my pride wants to scream, "Sorry, too late!" I think about turning down the proposal. I spend a lot of time wondering about what sacrifices I might make as a future coach's wife, especially juxtaposed to his unwillingness to sacrifice his own plan in service of mine, which I convince myself is ours. He gives up nothing about his plan. He waited until he secured a Division I coaching job before proposing. *Will his plan now be mine?*

Sacrifice is giving up something. Empathy is giving in.

His plan is now mine. I say *yes* the next morning, but my agreement comes with a handful of contingencies about how things can't always follow his plan, but must follow our shared plan, which will have to be one of equal compromise and equal sacrifice. It will be a plan that is organized and detailed with short- and long-term goals. Our marriage will be a union in which we both sacrifice for each other in order to execute the well thought-out master plan.

Unfortunately, our pre-marital counseling never really lines up with this. In fact, the bulk of our counseling addressed the dismantling of my concept for a detailed plan for our lives. "God is in control," pastor repeats. But it's difficult for me to reconcile the pastor's advice with the central idea I hold in my heart that shared sacrifice is the foundation of a happy marriage. After session number two, I have pre-marital counseling fatigue, and I just agree with everything the pastor throws our way about having a long-lasting marriage—communication, regular sex, joint banking accounts, and, of course, no over-planning. After each session, I look at Jeff and mouth, "Stick to the plan."

Marriage is simple. We got this!
I sacrifice for you, and you do the same. Deal? Deal.

In the year we plan our wedding, Jeff starts his career as a Division I basketball coach and we move to Pittsburgh. I justified the move to Pittsburgh a few months before our wedding as a sacrifice I needed to make in service of our marriage, so I packed my bags quickly and with a smile on my face. I think I shouldn't worry too much about it. Pittsburgh is close to Cincinnati, and I have cousins and friends who live there. I sold my home in Cincinnati, another willing sacrifice, and we purchased a new condo outside of Pittsburgh, five miles from IKEA and Robinson Mall. Although my commute to work is about fifty miles through Pennsylvania and West Virginia to Steubenville, Ohio, I am excited for new beginnings. I love working at Big Red High School, and I love being the wife of Coach Massey. I think, *Sacrifice is what it takes, and I got this.*

I took extra courses and sat for another certification exam for my Pennsylvania school counseling licensure just to have additional options and a sound back-up plan for our new life together. We are happily living together, both working in professions we love, and we have a solid plan for the future. I missed my friends and family, but I convinced any of them passing through Pennsylvania to stay the night, visit IKEA, in an effort to help me battle the loneliness I encounter with Jeff's travel schedule and work demands. With my newfound time, I learned new recipes and took on the executive chef position in our home, with no sous-chef in sight. *Sacrifice, right?* I'm not sure what Jeff is sacrificing at this point. But I'm okay with that. I was giving him time to settle into his new career, and was taking note of how much sacrificing he would need to do to catch up and even things out.

Actually, I only gave him eight months to settle. Spring comes, and my birthday month of April. I'm ready to embark on our master plan and I insist that we start trying to have a baby. By the end of April, we are expecting our first child. I was overwhelmed with excitement, ready to add some noise to our quiet condo, to gain more family visits since we'd have a cute baby to share, and I immediately started brainstorming which guest room might transition into a nursery. I can see in my mind just where the crib will go, the changing station, a chair next to a small dresser.

A short three weeks later, we find out there may not be a need to further discuss which room will be the new nursery. On a Friday afternoon, Jeff calls from work to tell me about "Coach," his boss and head coach, taking another job, and wanting to take Jeff with him. I stood there in the kitchen, with the phone in my hand, in disbelief. I am caught off guard once again. This time, it is not a glass of orange Kool-Aid, but it all feels the same. I have no idea how to respond.

Sacrifice is relinquishing your individual agenda. Empathy is retaining your shared promise.

Although I know moves are inevitable, part of a coach's lifestyle, I am not prepared for the spontaneity of the moves. We'd bought a beautiful condo less than a year before and were already faced with leaving it. Someone forgot to tell this new wife to check how long the head coach has left on his contract before buying a home. Jeff gives me vague details about the offer – his second coaching offer in nine months – over the phone and wants to talk more once he gets home, "in person." I know three things from our quick four-minute call: The head coach, Jeff's boss, is taking St. Bonaventure's head coaching position. He is not asking all of the assistant coaches to go with him, but he asked Jeff. Jeff's salary will triple.

I hang up the phone and anxiously await my newlywed husband to enter through our garage door. I have so many questions, but the biggest one is this: *is the salary increase really worth the move to Olean,*

New York? I am very familiar with St. Bonaventure University. I have traveled there twice during my college basketball career to play the Bonaventure Bonnies. It was always a dreaded road trip. This possible relocation is in the middle of nowhere, and I am not prepared to give up everything about my life. So, I formulate my contingencies just in case.

The garage door seems so much louder than usual when it opens. I hear Jeff get out of the car, close the car door, begin fumbling with his keys. I immediately open the door, anxiously awaiting his mood and more details. He walks in with a slight and easy smile, but I don't greet him. No kiss or small talk. I want to get right to it.

I'm surprised when I hear the excitement in Jeff's voice. The new conference league is considered a higher level. The prospective university signed a long-term contract with Jeff's boss, creating more stability for Jeff as an assistant coach. And my husband never expected to make such significant leaps in salary and competition in his first year at the Division I level.

On the other hand, I was not that excited. All I could think about were the sacrifices I had made and the new sacrifices I would have to make. *I don't have a New York school license. I don't have family in western New York. I don't have very many good memories of Olean. I hate the idea of finding a new home for our growing family.* I am overwhelmed with what I have to give up. So much so that I don't even acknowledge his visible excitement about the tripled salary. Rather, my response is a quick math lesson. I explain very dismissively that his new salary is comparable to our current combined salary, meaning if I don't find a job as a school counselor in this small town with less than 16,000 people, technically, there isn't any increase in salary for our household at all. Jeff nods his head and says he has to go to the bathroom. I think he cries in the bathroom. I'm pretty sure he is crying.

Jeff returns to the kitchen and acknowledges my concerns and future sacrifices, and validates my anxiety, reassuring me that this is, in fact, a joint decision. I'm surprised by this "joint decision" talk, so I quickly inquire about what his next steps will be if he doesn't take the offer. I know he hasn't thought about any other option but continuing to climb the coaching ladder. He confirms that he is unsure about what he would do instead of packing up and heading to New York. It's his uncertainty yet genuine willingness to figure out a contingency plan that moves me in the direction of sacrificing any further conversation about plan B. I know my husband. I know he wants to be a college coach. I know he does not want to give up his career so soon.

We recognize that there are no available coaching positions in Pittsburgh except for at Robert Morris, where he has been for the last nine months. In coaching, head coaches bring in their own staff. Rarely will they pick up an assistant coach who is already there, especially one that has only been there for one season. Nevertheless, this is a big, exciting career move that not all of the assistant coaches were offered. I reduce it to "following his plan." I show zero connection through excitement toward my husband. I am bombarded by the unevenness of sacrifices between us, and because of this, I am blinded to his attempts to empathize and connect with his new wife and the soon-to-be mother of his children.

Sacrifice is not empathy. Sacrifice is a byproduct of empathy.

Over and over again in our first four years of marriage, through two moves, a new baby, and several failed attempts at securing employment, Jeff continues to acknowledge my feelings. And it pisses me off. I'm not interested in his understanding of my feelings because I'm convinced that he can't understand them. Jeff doesn't know what it's like to be in my shoes. *He is not sacrificing nearly as much as I am.* He couldn't possibly imagine my fears about birthing a baby eight hours away from my family, in the middle of nowhere, surrounded by mountains and snow. There is no way for him to imagine how I feel, no way for him to feel my particular experience, and therefore, in my mind, there is no opportunity for him to understand the sacrifices I have made, since he hasn't. I give him little opportunity to demonstrate how much he cares about and understands my frustrations. I'm cold and unapproachable and resentful. Our master plan had been entirely supplanted by Jeff's career plan.

There is very little love expressed in our small orange home on Willow Street. I am angry and upset, and constantly tallying up my sacrifices. Jeff spends as much time in the gymnasium as he can to avoid the tallying. Sometimes I even need a break from myself. I need a break from the closing argument I'm constantly rehearsing in my head, from thinking about Jeff living his best life at my expense. Two and a half years pass, and in an effort to give myself a break from the resentment and anger embedded inside me, from retelling myself the same old stories about how *my life was not supposed to be this way*, I pick up antiquing. I reach out and begin to socialize with other women who have also relocated. I start volunteering at the local church, and making wedding bouquets out of fabric flowers and vintage brooches. It is what I can find to do in Olean to keep my mind occupied. And it is helpful. So is Jeff.

It turns out, I'm pretty crafty, like my mom. At one point, I pick up more weddings than I can manage by myself, so Jeff volunteers to help. It is in these moments, while he cuts circles of burlap, me sitting next to him on the floor, sewing the circles together, when we share in less emotionally charged conversations. For the first time in our marriage, I am not fixated on what I have given up while we discuss our thoughts and feelings. Jeff is unlikely to admit it, but he loves cutting circles with me because he enjoys helping me feel valued and productive once again. It is during these times that he is less overwhelmed with guilt. He shares with me as we talk in front of the piles of brooches and lace that his guilt increases with each rejection letter I receive from prospective counseling positions. He carries guilt about the money we are losing while not being able to sell our condo in Pittsburgh. I listen to his worries about being the sole provider in such a fickle coaching industry, and to my surprise, I finally hear that we share mutual fears about the future, that we carry the same regrets about the past, and we lay down the same exact frustrations about where it's best to educate our children.

We didn't give up how either of us felt. We gave in.

I just wanted Jeff to put himself in my shoes and sacrifice the same. I wanted him to take off his shoes, his plans, and even sacrifice his joy in the fruition of his plans, in order to put on my shoes, which were full of frustration. I wanted him to struggle in the same manner I was—walk in my shoes, feel what I was feeling. The miseducation of empathy implies we must commit this sacrificial act—that we must take off ourselves and step into another person's feelings. I was sure Jeff was *supposed* to do this for me.

Empathy is not a conditional response.

Jeff's empathy toward me is consistent, regardless of the intensity or degree of my behaviors, the way I continue to tally sacrifices, or my unwillingness to accept his understanding. He keeps his shoes on by remaining motivated and positive in his career while not allowing my feelings to overwhelm him. He rarely allows his emotions to match the intensity and condition of mine. Jeff is visibly very upset about me being upset, yet he continually validates how I am feeling by acknowledging how much harder it must be for me to be home all day with no adult interactions, loss of career, and adjusting to being a new mom. He opens the floor for me to express how I feel, even though I share the same heightened feelings over and over again. And during rare moments where I express beyond my feelings and share my thoughts – my beliefs about the future, my fears – he shares in those moments and connects with me—being first time parents, and being so far away from familiarity. He validates my feelings. He connects with our shared thoughts time and time again. And he does it unconditionally.

Although I had grown up in a home where my parents validated my feelings and inquired about what I was thinking in order to express their understanding, regardless of how emotional I was, I didn't practice what they had modeled for me. The way I connected the concept of marriage to an almost ritual belief in the importance of shared sacrifice got in the way of my logic. These new and intense feelings sprang up in me from feeling assigned to the role of "wife" and all I felt came with that, which seemed mostly like the sacrifice of my own plans. Regardless of my parents' teachings, the sociocultural understanding of empathy jaded my ability to truly empathize with my husband's needs and desires and accept his empathy toward me. So, I opted out of showing empathy for my husband altogether because of the condition I was in. I had made so many sacrifices in our short time of being married, there was no way I was going to add another tally mark; make another sacrifice by having to take my shoes off to put myself in his.

What Olean, New York, and all of the sacrifices that came with the move, taught me about my marriage and our desire to stay connected during transition and tough times is that sacrifice should be a byproduct of empathy. When shared connected understanding is not present in any relationship as the foundation, sacrifice will always be an act of reluctance and resentfulness that keeps score. But when you connect to another person by listening to the motives, beliefs, and thoughts behind their feelings, both people are given the opportunity - not the obligation - to make sacrifices for one another in response.

Empathy is what has kept my marriage from no longer being a running scoreboard of who has made the most sacrifices. Instead, our marriage is constant game film. In college basketball, coaches spend hours on end watching game film in an effort to sift out what play calls and schemes are working and which are not, who's providing quality minutes, and which lineup is playing well together - connected. They're looking for which players communicate well with each other and are so connected that they can anticipate, respond, and support their teammates' next move. Game film, like marriage, can be tedious, tiring, and exciting. Our marriage has seen many losses, overtime losses, and blow-out losses, too. Our marriage has also seen some close wins, and has come from behind upset victories, like Olean, NY. Empathy, not sacrifice, was the MVP that season.

CHAPTER TWO

Empathy is Not Sympathy

Your Sorry Makes Me Feel Sorry

I couldn't sleep the entire night. I think I'm experiencing Braxton Hicks pains. They are sharp jabs in my stomach, but I imagine contractions to be way worse. In the morning, I take a long shower in our studio apartment and begin to put my makeup on in preparation for my baby shower, hosted by the coaches wives. It starts in a few hours. Many of the wives are from other sports teams at St. Bonaventure and I have not yet met them. I am excited to meet them and eat cake. I struggle with the sharp pains piercing in my side as I try not to poke my eye with liner. I suddenly have the urge to pee and hit the toilet. Minutes later, I realize the long stream that lasts much longer than a pee is likely my water breaking. I sit there and I begin to pray.

From the day I found out I would be a mother, I have prayed the same prayer: that God keep us safe, let my baby be healthy, and that she be free of vitiligo – a skin disease that plagued my own childhood. Vitiligo causes patches on the skin where pigmentation is lost, and because of this, it is typically more noticeable on darker skin, presenting as white patches on the hands, face, and other parts of the body. Usually, vitiligo happens at birth. You know right away. But my case is a very rare one, triggered right before puberty. I pray my daughter won't have it, too.

For me, it happens at age eleven. I wake up to small white patches on my face that grow bigger before quickly spreading over my body the summer before sixth grade. It is devastating, and the constant specialist and doctor visits interrupt my summers at the neighborhood pool and soccer practice with my team.

Our frequent family gatherings are altered as well. They're no longer filled with laughter or my cousins running in and out of the screen door, the wood frame slamming behind them. The women in my family hug me tight while they cry and pray for a miraculous healing. Our conversations become consumed with which medicine I'm trying and which doctor I will see next. Now, with big white patches on my face, arms and legs, my presence changes the mood instantaneously.

I can feel everyone's sorrow for me. The people I know and love are unabashed in their grief. For those who don't know me, it's the same sorrow mixed with curiosity. It is, indeed, a sad turn of events—one minute I'm flashing my smile with one hand on my hip in front of any camera pointing my way, and a summer later I am running from any camera that might be able to snap my picture. I don't want to have a photo that makes everyone sad, even when I am not in the room. When I look in the mirror as a young girl, I am mostly in shock and disbelief. I don't believe my own reflection, and I begin to conflate what I see with sadness itself. I am sadness. People see sadness when they look at me, and I feel sadness on the inside.

I avoid going outside and seeing the neighborhood kids I once played with - always until the streetlights came on. I just don't want anyone to express sadness for me. I don't want pity, and I don't want to be asked questions I have no answers for. *Why did I get it? How did I get it? Will it ever go away?* I just want to be myself. After a few weeks of having vitiligo, I am used to the stares I get from other kids, and how adults quickly look away from me. You would expect me to feel bad when small children scream as they make eye contact with me in the grocery store, but what actually makes me feel bad is when their parents are visibly embarrassed by this and apologize for their child's response to me. That's all it ever is. Just an apology. Adults always made me feel like I needed help, needed saving, needed a miracle.

My protective mother exhausted herself trying to help me; trying to, I suspect, relieve her sadness. She felt sorry that I had to endure the stares and screams of little kids, so she took me out of town to get matched for special dermatological makeup that was thick and messy but that could cover the white patches. But the makeup only brings more attention to my skin – to my weirdness – and it requires us to spend hours trying to fuss with and apply something to fix me, like a bruised fruit or a broken doll. By summer's end, I insist on starting school without the makeup. My friends have questions, I have very few answers, and my face is the conversation for just a day. That day was worth it, because afterwards life went on and the conversation switched to more normal things, like Andre finally admitting to liking Dorothy and who knew all the lyrics to Karen White's ballad, *I'm Not Your Superwoman*. Ronald, the annoying boy who professed his love for me in second grade, third grade, fourth grade, and fifth also professes his love for me the first week of sixth grade, despite my new appearance.

I only wear makeup to school once in the winter on picture day. I wish I hadn't. My peers smile and stare when I walk in the room, and my teacher must have mentioned something to our principal about my new look because she pulled me out of the room early that day. My principal closed the classroom door behind me, smiling, as we both stood in the hallway. Because of her smile, I know I'm not in trouble, but I have no idea what caused this impromptu visit. She leans forward with a big grin and says, "Did your mom do your makeup? Because it looks 100% better." And then she hugs me, causing the makeup to rub on her white shirt. I just stood there as she opened the door for me to return to class. *100% better.* Adults were striking out, badly.

I do not want any of this for my new baby girl. And because of my genes, it is possible for her to acquire it, too. It is really my only concern with having my first child – not the pain I will endure with every push, not her physical health, not that she is coming a few weeks early, but that she might have imperfections in her skin that cause people, mostly grown adults, to show her sympathy.

January 13th, 2008, I gave birth to Aubrey Jane, a healthy little peanut with beautiful caramel, perfectly even skin. I am so relieved and able to enjoy the celebratory texts and videos of women playing baby shower games without me coming through my phone as I hold my new baby. Four years later, I would repeat the same prayer for my second girl. She is born in September, with beautiful chocolate, perfectly even skin. All seems well, and I tell myself that I will save my worry for when Aubrey and Kayla turn eleven, the year that my perfectly even brown skin began to turn white.

I should have prayed for the banishment of all the dermatological autoimmune diseases possible, and then not waited until each of them turned eleven. Aubrey is eight years old and Kayla just turned four. Every two weeks, I wash and detangle Kayla's thick, curly hair. But this time, as I am complaining about the three-hour process, I find a bald spot the size of a dime on the crown of her head. I commit to detangling more often in an effort to prevent another bald spot. For three consecutive Sundays, I watch the spot get bigger and bigger, and decide to reach out to hairstylists and dermatologists to find out what's going on. Through bloodwork and allergy testing, and months of running from homeopathologists to dermatologists, we finally reach a diagnosis of Alopecia Universalis. In a matter of five months, my four-year-old girl loses her eyebrows, eyelashes, and all of her hair on her head. And I lose my peace.

The amount of guilt that I feel is indescribable. *Why did I risk putting my children through what I went through? Faces of sadness and years of insecurity. Why didn't I stop at one child? Why didn't I intervene sooner and more aggressively when I saw the first bald spot? What did I feed or expose her to that triggered her little immune system to attack her hair? I should have been more careful with her diet knowing she is predisposed to autoimmune skin diseases.* I am now the woman in the family constantly crying and praying as I hug my daughter. And although she is only four, like me at age eleven, she doesn't want to be around my sadness and is wondering if she has done something wrong.

Sympathy, in many cases, expresses confusion, not understanding.

I easily recognize Kayla's bob and weave away from sympathy. It is all too familiar to me. She gravitates towards friends who are extra jovial and, whenever possible, leaves the room if people start crying, praying, or hugging me in an attempt to offer comfort. Her older sister does a better job of hiding her tears from Kayla and is a refuge of laughs, board games, and giggles. But I usually can't fight away the tears. I am in need of comfort. With each rollercoaster of regrowth and relapse, I endure the emotional ups and downs of hope, despair, and guilt. I see my mother's face, and I see powerlessness when I look in the mirror.

Alopecia can be cyclical, and different interventions work for different people. So here I am, on the same quest as my mother, trying any- and everything to fix my baby girl. I try diets. No gluten, no dairy, no oats, no sugar, all for a four-year-old girl who loves Swedish fish and pizza. Rogaine, creams, steroid shots. Prayer, fasting, and the anointed oil I believe caused my own miraculous recovery from the white patches covering my face becomes my most frequent intervention. I am trying to remain faithful that the same God can work on Kayla's behalf. I am exhausted. Fragile. Frustrated. It's hard reliving what I experienced as a little girl.

Family and friends, out of love, don't realize how delicate my spirit really is. In their attempt to support, love and comfort me, they mostly miss the mark. It is hard to sit and listen and validate my feelings when you are consumed with your own. I know they are overwhelmed with their own feelings of sadness as they look at my little girl's bald head – the same head that used to be covered in long curls. You can see it in their eyes and when they shake their head in disbelief. It's hard for them to be present and not become enmeshed in my immense guilt. They are not used to seeing me like this. In this season, I am no longer an optimistic, sarcastic, positive, laughing mother. I am in desperate need of empathy, but I mostly get what I got as a kid. "I'm sorry." Everyone's so sorry.

Small glimpses of empathy keep me connected while swimming in a sea of sympathy. They keep me out of isolation. Real empathy sticks out to me because it's the only thing that doesn't make me feel like I did something horribly wrong, and I discover it when it becomes the core of a conversation I have with a fellow coach's wife and mom.

Instead of saying, "I am so sorry," she starts off with, "You are so strong." She recognizes that she is unfamiliar with how I must feel and doesn't attempt to imagine it. She listens and validates what I am feeling, and it's hard for her to do – hard to listen to the defeat in my voice – but she keeps her shoes on and walks alongside me. I feel heard and understood, and I don't feel like an unexpected rainstorm who dampens the mood.

About eight months after losing all of her hair, Kayla began to grow it back. The growth was slow and steady, and so was my hope. Her tiny head becomes nearly covered with more manageable, looser curls than before. I am aware of a possible relapse, but I'm optimistic about God's healing power – until I see a small spot in the middle of a patch of new growth. I am nervous, and I should be.

Three weeks after noticing the small bald spot, eight months of hair is gone again. I am tired. And there is no ounce of faith left in me. Those who are close to me sense it, too. Especially my friend Bobbi.

I don't know if it was a vague Facebook post or my numbness at Kayla's dance practice, but Bobbi noticed. Normally, all the dance moms sit together in the waiting room and watch our little ballerinas through the flatscreen. It was fun to dote over our daughters together, to laugh about the way they made up their own moves whenever they forgot the routine, to connect with other moms. But coming to grips with Kayla's alopecia and the lifelong uncertainty it created for her had taken its toll on me. Bobbi could sense that, and she immediately text me after practice to schedule a meetup. I reluctantly agreed. I was so fragile, and Bobbi was the last person I wanted to make sad.

I first met Bobbi through my neighborhood family group. She is a sweet spirit who lives life to the fullest. I think this about Bobbi because she is a joy to be around – one of those infectious types who is always smiling and who has a big laugh you want to hear. I'm attracted to her fashion sense, her positivity, and the general lack of sadness in her world. She is a beam of light for me, so I was shocked when a mutual friend of ours disclosed to me that Bobbi was living with stage four lung cancer. I was in complete disbelief, but it's this fact about Bobbi – the way she seems to understand things about life, about happiness – that guides me through my own feelings.

At the time, Bobbi is in the midst of traveling between different cities for treatments, and yet she wants to meet up with me. I know my friend wants to check in and be a support, but I'm worried about an encounter with sympathy.

We settle on a Thursday afternoon to get together. Bobbi brings wine and chocolate over to my home, plops down, and asks for an update on Kayla. I think I got through two sentences before tears began to roll down my cheeks. I cry and she listens. I share my frustrations about failed treatments and diets, relapses, and my inability to fix it permanently. She understands and acknowledges those same thoughts. "An inability to fix it permanently."

I pause. *That's right, she must have these same thoughts,* I think to myself. But she is not thinking about hair. She is thinking about cancer, and that feels much bigger, putting things into a different perspective.

Bobbi never makes me feel guilty for having all of these big feelings toward a non-terminal autoimmune disease. She doesn't outmatch my concerns with her own about her daughter's ability to cope with her cancer diagnosis. In the midst of my pouring out, I frequently pause mid-sentence as I am smacked in the face with the irony of her being there for me.

"I worry about Kayla's future. Will she go to prom?" I pause. It is a long, awkward pause. I think of Bobbi's daughter, Kate, and if Bobbi will even be able to witness her daughter attending prom. I am silent in complete embarrassment. Bobbi smiles, raises her glass, shoves me my glass, and tells me to take another drink. Our ensuing long conversation is a back-and-forth tennis match of validation of feelings and the acknowledgement of a mutual understanding about our thoughts and beliefs and even wavering spiritual beliefs. She makes sure to gently hit the ball, making it easier for me to connect and return it back at the same pace. I follow her lead because her lead confirms what I'm discovering about connection and empathy and how differently it looks than sympathy. It is what I'd needed ever since I was eleven years old.

Sympathy can appear lethargic in comparison to empathy. For example, "I'm so sorry for your loss" is a very acceptable and common sympathetic response to death. It is appropriate because it is a deposit of care and concern, but empathy goes further. Empathy takes the time to consider a whole person and why they feel they way they do, creating a larger understanding and a deep connection.

Sympathy is a deposit of concern. Empathy is an investment that accrues interest beyond concern.

Bobbi went beyond feeling sorry for me. She would quickly ignore my apologies for venting about what I thought was insignificant in comparison to what she was personally enduring, and quickly invest her attention back to me. In between her own treatments, she checked in on me and my daughter, wiped away the tears I shed for hours, researched and referred me to specialists and doctors, and regularly stopped by the boutique I owned with wine and gifts. Based on the time we spent laughing and smiling, I'm hopeful that her expression of empathy and connection was just as healing for her as it was for me. Thank you, Bobbi. You reminded me of my mother's ability to connect, without comparison or judgement. I miss your light.

CHAPTER THREE

Empathy is Not Vicarious Feelings

College and the Search for Connection

My mother and father taught me the true meaning of empathy, then my formal education distorted it.

I watched my father kiss and hug my mother when he walked in the door every evening after work. I listened to my mother pour out stories about her workday to Dad as she cuddled against his large six-foot-four frame on the couch. Dad was always complimenting Mom's cooking and bragged about her career accomplishments constantly. He hardly ever said no to any of her requests, and he was always the first one to call a truce when they got in disagreements.

Mom was a superwoman, balancing extensive travel for work and her family, her acts of love were visible and constant. I watched my parents build and grow, conquer adversities, play off each other's strengths, and step in for each other's weaknesses. Dad was a calculated risk-taker and an introvert. Mom was the opposite. Whenever there was a promotion or an opportunity to move up professionally, Mom applied. In the same manner, she pushed Dad to try new things, adventures, and consider professional mobility. At the same time, Dad knew exactly when to step in and convince Mom to slow down and rest.

Our home was filled with conversations, but rarely consumed by overt expressions of emotions or feelings, except for when my brother and I were in our teenage years. My parents would validate our feelings and then quickly question the thoughts behind them. Consequently, I had to adjust once I started playing basketball because I realized screaming coaches didn't really want to know – literally – what I was thinking when I turned the ball over. In my home, there was less time devoted to how you felt, and more time devoted to uncovering your thoughts.

I didn't truly realize that my upbringing might have been different than others' until college. I was thrust into a coed dorm full of emotions, all spilling out from everyone around me. I noticed right away that I made decisions differently than anyone else, I handled adversity more strategically, and I held less grudges than most around me. My feelings weren't in the driver's seat.

But if I'm being honest, my feelings weren't necessarily in the backseat all the time either, as is to be expected with such a big transition accompanied by so many changes. My first two years of college found me trying to adjust as a student athlete with my feelings sitting right in the passenger seat, but I did everything in my power not to let them drive. My emotions tried on several occasions, but I did what my parents modeled and focused on not giving my feelings the wheel. The more I witnessed relationships and interactions in college, the more I became conscious of how driving my car with my thoughts made it easier for me to adjust to college life.

It was clear that emotions were driving my friends' relationships from one argument to the next.

From bleach being thrown in full closets to students walking out of class and back to the dorm to pack their things up (and their full academic scholarships with them), never to return to campus again because of how they felt while being the only student of color in most of their classes.

My friends and teammates who were less driven by their feelings also appeared to connect and get along with a diversity of people and a variety of circumstances. They forgave easily and resolved conflicts seamlessly. They were simply more empathetic towards others. Their emotions did not distract them from connecting, and they expressed understanding of why others were feeling the way they were feeling because they were able to focus on what the other person was thinking.

It is during this time at Xavier University that I realize how different I am and how very few people connect the way I do. The majority of girls are uncertain about connecting with me. I think differently about empathy and connection, and it shows. Never trying to walk in others' shoes or share in the experience of their emotions, I am not embraced by the women I see gathered together with popcorn and Zima, sharing in the miseries of break-ups, crushes, and homesickness. I have a very different outlook that is often interpreted as insensitive and interrogative.

This is something I didn't experience in high school – during which I was consumed by trying to balance sports, my studies, and my high school sweetheart. Because of this, I made little time for girlfriends outside of my teammates, so college was supposed to be a welcomed fresh start. But I couldn't have accounted for the way I was taught to understand connection and empathy. Empathy just looks different on me.

I never knew how much I desired a posse outside of sports until the summer leading into my first year of college. After high school graduation, I often heard my fellow graduates referring to "the last summer" – the last summer before their forever friendships would be stretched and tested; the last summer before many people moved away. Secretly, I wanted to express this same sentiment after college, because I hadn't felt the fleeting loss of friendships. Therefore, I set out to build forever friendships outside of my new teammates that could last once I left Xavier University.

Four other freshmen joined me in starting our athletic careers for the Lady Musketeer basketball team. Four of us were from Ohio and the other from Helsinki, Finland. It is highly recommended by our coaches that freshmen live with each other, and so we do. I was excited to hear that athletes who room together have the luxury of moving in a couple of weeks earlier than the general student body. I had so many ideas for the décor of our room. And it turns out that Krista doesn't seem to mind my ideas, which is a good thing.

I met Krista upon walking into the room with my mom and eight-year-old brother. My dad was following in tow, hugging boxes full of high school team pictures and posters of Michael Jordan. Krista's things were already unpacked, and her family was preparing to leave to get a bite to eat. We hit it off instantly. I immediately like Krista. Our families met when they crossed paths in the hallway, and the conversation sounds like that of proud parents, gushing over our athletic accolades.

For the first few weeks, Krista and I sit on our beds in front of a small TV that softly plays *Martin* each night as we talk about how nervous we are, about adjusting to a new coach, new teammates, and new routines of practicing, traveling, and living together. Fellow athletes tell us that the transition to college basketball is very difficult. With dial-up internet and email just being introduced on campus, most of our efforts to get class notes, make-up assignments, and to reschedule quizzes and exams from missed days for away games is something we have to make plans for right away.

Our athletic advisor, the infamous Sister Roseann, a quiet and persistent five-foot nun who lives in the same on-campus apartment building as our junior and senior men's basketball players, tells us to make friends with responsible students in class who will attend regularly, and not to forget the small tape recorder we were provided with to record classes.

Sister encourages us to be pleasant with the professors in spite of many who are resentful that our education is being paid for because of how well we can dribble a basketball.

Krista and I talk about how distant and distracted the upperclassmen appear to be. We are an unusually big freshman class of five coming in, and the first class with a foreign player and two Black players, now tallying up to a grand total of three—the most the school has ever had. We learn our team will be playing in a new, more competitive league of the Atlantic-10 conference, but we don't even have a coaching staff secured. Days after arriving, it is announced that our head coach, who recruited all of us freshman to play for him, is leaving for another school down the road in Toledo, Ohio. While the athletic department is in search of a new coach, it seems like yesterday that Coach was in my living room, eating my mom's pork steaks and macaroni and cheese, as he offered me an opportunity to play for him at Xavier University.

The coach who recruited me knew my shortcomings and still believed in my potential, so I was mainly nervous about my ability to play at the college level, and the new coach finding out. I think Krista shared in some of the same nervousness. We talk a lot about who will replace him. *Will they be a male or a female? Will they be a yeller? Sarcastic? All business or personable? Will they be patient or will they just assign an assistant coach to be patient with us?* Krista and I were validating each other's feelings and connecting in our shared thoughts.

Krista definitely missed home more than I did. My mother wouldn't let me miss anything and insisted that I go home every weekend. Xavier University was a little less than thirty minutes away from my home. And she kept showing up on her lunch hour to drop off food and anything else she could think of. Conversely, Krista stayed on the phone all the time, talking to her family, talking to her friends back home, and to a particular boy who she giggles with all hours of the night. I didn't mind because we only had one landline in the dorm, so when Krista was on the phone, my mother could only reach a busy signal. This created a little bit of distance between the constant – and mostly unexpected – visits, like when the RA let my mother in so she could hand-deliver collard greens directly to my door. Thank goodness my room was clean, and that I was actually studying, alone, without any boys in the room. Krista and I were able to laugh about my mom's tight grip on her first-born baby girl, and we learn even more about each other with every late-night chat.

Neither of us are good at getting up in time to have breakfast, or to walk calmly over to Schmidt Fieldhouse for 6 a.m. practice. Instead, we both hit snooze until our phones start ringing – our trainer, Jodi, screaming on the other end. Krista and I both sprint out of the door, down the hill, and across the street to the gym – just in time for practice. The season is underway. We had a new coach who was very confident in the style of play she introduced to us, and how it will win games. I believe in her style. However, I don't believe in my abilities to play this style. Krista was more confident than me, until her knee became more and more of a problem. After further investigation, our trainers determine that she has a tear and needs surgery, which Krista gets immediately in the first month of school.

Krista is apprehensive about the surgery, but she goes through with it and is out for the next several months. Although Krista is hurt, we still spend a lot of time together in Schmidt Fieldhouse and back in our dorm room on the second floor of Kuhlman Hall. She doesn't talk too much about her injury – about her first surgery or the next surgery she needs in January – and I don't bring it up. I listen as she periodically complains about the brace, treatment, and rehab in the training room, but it's hard to know what she's feeling or her thoughts surrounding them. In my entire life playing sports, I'd never been hurt – not even a sprained ankle. I have seen plenty of nasty injuries happen before my eyes on the basketball court, the soccer field, and in the lanes of hurdles on the track, but I can't imagine what it feels like. But our room was a safe place for her to express how she was feeling. I just think we were both overwhelmed with intense feelings and wanted to connect in other ways - lighter ways.

Oddly, I hear some relief in Krista's voice about being on the sidelines and not on the court with the new coach, with new plays, new expectations, and new frustrations. Our juniors and seniors are not too receptive to our new coach's style of play and they express it during practice often. Instead of basketball, Krista and I constantly talk about something we both share equally: "not being a regular student" and craving socialization outside of basketball. Sports teams create an atmosphere of camaraderie, but being part of a team can feel like a forced obligation, full of orchestrated connections. And too many times, it isn't enough. It wasn't enough for me or Krista.

Homesickness combined with Krista's knee injury had her leaving nearly every weekend for home visits, too, just before she began talking about transferring to a university closer to home, with "more familiar faces." Like Krista, I spent the first couple of months contemplating, almost daily, transferring not only to another school but to another sport; the sport I am more confident in, more familiar with, and mostly for which I was recruited to play at the collegiate level. Soccer. But Krista and I both stay to fulfill our commitments and continue to brace the impact of being a first-year Division I student-athlete together. We spent that year connected in providing each other with what we thought was best and safe.

I've been a soccer player since I was seven, and started basketball twice as old at fourteen – my first year in high school. Basketball was a new and exciting sport that I loved learning. I excelled with every move I picked up - so much so that I was recruited during my last year in high school as a basketball "project," mainly because of my fast footwork and the coordination I'd developed on the soccer field. But there isn't enough footwork in the world for me to catch up to the skillset of my teammates – a skillset they'd been developing for as long as I'd been playing soccer. Many practices, I stay in Schmidt Fieldhouse gym as my teammates leave, one by one, finishing up their made-ten free throws in a row before heading back to the dorms. I stood on the free throw line, with an angry assistant coach contemplating whether to just lie and say I made all ten so she could go home or to be honest and stay with me for the extra two to three hours it took until I could finally make all ten shots in a row.

It is a year of feeling behind on the basketball court; of feeling alone and isolated. I hesitate to share any of these feelings – to tell anyone I don't feel like

I fit in or like I measure up – because of the guilt that engulfs me. I don't give myself permission to have these feelings of embarrassment and inadequacy. As soon as I felt these feelings come to the surface, I would rattle off a rebuttal percentage in my head, reminding myself of how few high school athletes could earn a full-ride scholarship to play Division I basketball and how fortunate I was. I remind myself of how many other *better* high school basketball players invested hours upon countless hours to perfect their shot since starting as young as six, seven, eight – not fourteen, like me.

I was blessed enough to earn $30,000 a year to acquire a top-notch education at a prestigious Jesuit university based on my potential, not my current abilities; based on what I might be able to do, not what other high school players had done. There was no way I would allow myself permission to feel all the things I was feeling. I was afraid it would come off as ungrateful. I didn't have an injury that sidelined me for the season and I wasn't ever worried about how I was going to pay for my chemistry book. I dared not express my feelings to my mom, who wore Xavier gear almost every weekend after I signed my letter of intent. I don't bother to reach out to Amber, one of my sweetest friends and AAU basketball teammate from high school who is playing a few blocks away at the University of Cincinnati and also trying to adjust to new teammates, new coaches, a bigger city, and way bigger classes than mine. I bury the feelings of how upset and betrayed I feel being left to fail by the coach who recruited me, and the immediate guilt that follows for feeling this way.

Guilt is the thief of validation.

When you are misled into looking for connection and understanding rooted in sharing emotions, it causes you to hesitate in sharing certain feelings for fear of being rejected a connection. I'm convinced this was a barrier for me and Krista in sharing more. If each of us have to share in each other's emotions on top of already being consumed with our own for the sake of connection, we will just stick with our safe feelings and thoughts. This left me with more need for connection and understanding throughout my first year.

November came extremely fast. We were preparing for games, spending more time practicing and lifting weights, and I found myself devoting most of my spare moments to basketball. I'm reminded of this when I pass by groups of girls on my way home from practice, laughing and chatting on the lawn. I smile and say *hello*. I really just needed more time to be included. I walk slowly around clusters of girls giggling in the doorway next to the RA desk each night I return back to my room, and I make sure to listen and comment when there is a seamless opportunity. I say *yes* when invited to sit with a group of girls in the cafeteria, knowing that I just committed to a three-hour dinner after a long day of class and practice. Throughout my first year in college, I didn't instantly become a member of any regular group other than the Lady Musketeer basketball team—this fate seemed inescapable despite my efforts. A few laughs here, a gossip session there, moments sprinkled among the longest seven-month basketball season of my life.

I promised myself that I would find my tribe during sophomore year. Now that I knew the demands of basketball, I figured I could better schedule out time for a close group of friends outside of basketball. Living in the new dorms of Buenger Hall, even with mostly teammates, would give me that opportunity. The "new dorms," as we called them, weren't necessarily new but they were the newest on campus. Most of the rooms were suites made up of two or four bedrooms and a living area with two bathrooms. These dorms were perfect for girl talk, dance competitions, movie nights, and other shenanigans. My sophomore year would be a fresh start in the perfect dormitory, even without my freshman roommate, Krista, who does follow through and transfers to a new university. I still jump all in.

I took advantage of open room doors and invited myself into loud conversations from familiar voices from freshman year. I gather up friends to go eat on my fully loaded meal card at The Grill, the campus restaurant. I organize roller skating outings at the local rink a few blocks from campus. After all, Xavier is adjacent to my beloved childhood neighborhood of Bond Hill. The start of my sophomore year looks promising and my circle begins to form. I connect with girls who have similar interests, besides sports and dating male basketball players. My future tribe talks a lot. And so do I. My future tribe expresses their emotions – a lot of emotions. And so do I. But then they do this thing where they share in each other's emotions. That is unfamiliar to me. That I do not do. And I am the only one who doesn't. I remember thinking that maybe if I joined a sorority, I would figure out how to do this.

I heard a lot of commotion one Saturday morning, coming from the living area of my dorm. I slowly get out of bed as I overhear several different scenarios being discussed by my roommates – scenarios that possibly led up to the "crazy" episode that happened the night before. The conversation literally sounds like an episode of *Snapped*. I open my bedroom door slowly and listen, trying to determine if the conversation is worth getting out of bed for on my day off from practice. When one girl screeches because another said someone doused their roommate's closet in bleach, I decide it might be worth getting out of bed for. I walk into the living room to get the 411.

Rumor had it that the incident occurred between two of our friends from the first floor. My closet was mostly made up of basketball gear, crop tops and jeans, so it was hard for me to connect with the others about what a travesty it was the victim had lost *so many cute outfits*. I just wanted to know who the bleach-thrower was. I had other questions and thoughts that I kept to myself, though, and returned back to bed for a little more sleep. But the conversation in the living area does not allow me extra time with my pillow. They're loud and I can't drown out the high pitch of their voices no matter how many blankets I pile over my head, so I throw on sweats and boots and head to The Grill to get a Ms. Mickey special breakfast plate.

Ms. Mickey was every Black student's mom in the kitchen away from home. My plan is to return to my room with bacon, grits, eggs, and toast piled to the top of a white Styrofoam container, crawl back in bed, savor my eggs - cooked perfectly over easy - and marathon binge *Law and Order*.

Upon my return, carrying my stuffed Styrofoam container, I pass the room where the bleach incident took place. The door was slightly cracked, and I heard enough familiar voices to get up the nerve to knock. I'm wondering if my roommates made it downstairs and are on the other side of the door. They're not. They are likely still upstairs, still piecing together what they think happened. "Everybody okay? I heard what happened," I softly announce as I slowly walk in the room.

I knew when I walked in who the bleach-thrower was. I could tell by her demeanor and the way she quickly questioned me about what I'd heard. I shared the bits and pieces in less than two sentences, then closed the door behind me as I entered and started in on my food before it could get cold. As they go over the minutiae of the incident, debating the details, I can hear anger and sadness in their voices as the tension in the room begins to mount. When one person expresses anger, everybody becomes angry, and I watch as this emotional chain reaction recycles itself around the room. I don't absorb that anger or sadness. I actually don't say anything at all, because I can read the room here. They expect each other to empathize in a very specific way – in a way that's supposed to make them feel what the bleach-thrower feels. But I can't help myself from wondering what the girl who threw the bleach must've thought and felt. I wonder about both sides of the incident – the victim *and* the perpetrator – and I think that the girl who threw the bleach must have felt pretty mad or hurt to do such a thing. Everyone present is emotionally charged. I chime in, carefully.

"After hearing all of this, I think you have every right to be angry. I'd be pissed, too."

With this comment, I am part of the conversation. I'm connected. I'm still welcome. But I'm just a comment away from no longer being connected or welcome. Thoughtfully, I slide in a series of questions, intermittently, asking the perpetrator – the bleach-thrower – about her thoughts on the betrayal, her thoughts about the "other girl." I ask her what she said to herself leading up to grabbing the bottle of bleach. I ask too many questions. And I ask questions that don't want to be answered.

"So, now it's her fault?" The girls around me ask this in unison, the pitch of their voices in sync with accusatory shock.

"No, no, that's not what I'm saying. I just have had those thoughts before, too. The thought that, somehow, if I hurt the person who hurts me, it will make me feel better, but in the end, it only does for a few moments. It doesn't change the betrayal I felt, and then I feel worse about everything in the end. "

Nods of agreement silently bobbed from the girls in the room, but their lackluster approval wasn't enough to salvage the trust and connection I'd lost. And for many of the girls, my comments deemed me "judgmental." As I find a safe exit plan to leave the conversation and walk back to my room, I'm reminded how often this type of interaction happens to me, even with my teammates, my roommates, and my forming circle of friends. Although I acknowledge how people are feeling while consciously attempting not to judge, I don't necessarily feel what others are feeling as they express their emotions. And I tend to investigate more about what others are thinking in an effort to connect with and understand them – to empathize with them. This is what I yearned for from my teammates, coaches and friends. I didn't want anyone to share in my feelings of inadequacy, disappointment, betrayal, frustration, or grief. Mine was enough all by itself. I just wanted someone to give me permission to feel all these feelings, even with my unlimited meal card, good health, book voucher, and the trips to Alaska with my teammates. I wanted them to validate my feelings, share some understanding in the thoughts behind those feelings, regardless of their personal scenario, and connect with me. I wanted empathy. I didn't want anyone to have to walk in my shoes. I didn't want anyone to have to feel what I was feeling.

My second year of college was the beginning of my evolving understanding about how these moments of what appear to be disconnections for me can actually be more than a dry sense of humor, a different set of interests, or a personality conflict, but also maybe a reflection of the miseducation of empathy. Expression of empathy can look different than sharing emotions, and if you are not one who subscribes to the traditional expression of empathy, it may be more difficult to feel understood and make long-lasting close friends.

CHAPTER FOUR

Empathy is Not Innate

What the Streets of Bond Hill Taught Me

In my all-white Adidas shoes, I rode my bike for miles. In my jelly shoes, I played hopscotch and jump rope with my childhood friend almost daily. The neighborhood kids, in their Reebok pump sneakers, ran freely, watching for cars and the city Metro bus as it flew down the street, almost never stopping at the bus stop sign two doors down from my home. Walking a mile in my shoes meant walking through my beloved neighborhood of Bond Hill, right in the middle of Cincinnati, Ohio—a village of extended family, extra sets of "adopted" parents, ever-present

invitations to *stay for dinner*, and a gang of play cousins.
My childhood was filled with long summer nights of
cards, board games, and Jacks on designated porches;
hair straightening with hot combs carefully placed
on the stove in the specified neighborhood kitchens
where you were less likely to get burned on the ears;
hair braiding in the select living rooms that had cable
and the "good snacks," so you could endure the long
hours of sitting during the careful parting of your
hair and the placement of aluminum foil at the end of
each braid to keep the patterned color beads in place.
Claudine and I, and quite a few other girls, with our
shoes off, of course, got our hair braided in my living
room. It was the designated braid house.

I was six years old when my mom and dad
purchased a small white home on Berkley Avenue.
The home is only a few streets away from our last
apartment, but this street is special. This street has a
girl similar in age to me who lives right across from
us. I met Claudine the day after we moved in. I was
sitting on the porch when she ran over to warn me
that our street had more boys than girls, but not to
worry because, to make up for that, we have Mr. and
Mrs. Richardson on our street.

Mr. and Mrs. Richardson are affectionately known by all of the neighborhood kids as Aunt Helen and Uncle Bill. They are the only white couple on our block, and likely the street. I soon found out they were missionaries, and that Uncle Bill hosts a religious radio station down in his basement. When I met them, I instantly understood why we were so lucky to live on the same street, in spite of all the boys who run our hood. Aunt Helen and Uncle Bill have the only garage filled with pringles, the "government" block cheese, and cans of Hawaiian punch, plus more to pass out to various shelters around the city. Uncle Bill shared his garage goodies with us and the families on our block. He would place a brown paper bag full of groceries in your one hand and a mayonnaise and tomato sandwich wrapped in a paper towel in the other.

And then there was his wife, sweet Aunt Helen. Aunt Helen was the reason all of the kids on my street knew how to swim. On early mornings in the summer, a bunch of us piled in their station wagon and rode to the Jewish community center for swim lessons taught by Aunt Helen. She is also the reason we knew all of the books of the Bible. Less of us jump in the station wagon for vacation bible school, but Claudine and I sit in the back seat together, in our church shoes.

I jump in because Claudine always jumps in their station wagon. And I want to be wherever she is. In fact, she also jumps in her own bed, in her own bedroom at Aunt Helen and Uncle Bill's home, too, when she chooses not to stay at her house. It is a big room she helped decorate with full-time access to the garage, basement, and kitchen cupboard full of shiny packages of Grippo's potato chips and gigantic jars of peanut butter. I want to be in Claudine's shoes and have an extra bedroom in the Richardson's home, too – until my mother sits me down and tells me why Claudine has the second pink bedroom. It isn't always safe for Claudine in her home.

I don't want to feel what she is feeling.
As an eight-year-old, I can't walk in her shoes,
even if I knew the road she endured.

I heard my mom, yet Claudine having her own room in the popular Richardson's home still makes me feel less loved and less special. Regardless, I still want my friend with me at all times, so every weekend, I beg my parents for Claudine to spend the night. When Claudine slept at my house, I never felt less loved than her. It always felt like an equal playing field for both of us in my home. Even when I felt envious of my friend, or whenever Claudine felt sad about home, my parents didn't show her any pity, nor me any favoritism. We were equally treated as their daughters. No extra scoop of ice cream in her bowl or exemption for her setting the table! And absolutely no unfair "house rules" for when we played Nintendo. Nope! We were treated like sisters. We shared a connection to my parents and with each other in the midst of our feelings.

However, this vibe is not the same in our neighbors' homes. Adults don't treat Claudine like my parents do. Sitting on Ms. Betty's porch, playing Monopoly, several adults ask my friend how she's doing while shaking their heads from side to side in disappointment before Claudine can even respond. They offer her food and clothing that she makes clear she doesn't want or need. She is embarrassed by these overzealous encounters and wants to escape back to my home, to my parents.

How I treated Claudine didn't come naturally to me.
I treated my friend the way I saw my parents treat her,
and the way they treated me.

When I was eleven years old, on Christmas morning, I woke up with great hopes of receiving my first ten-speed bike. It was still pitch-black outside, but I thought it was close enough to morning to declare it was time to get started opening some presents. I was convinced I would find a new purple and gold bicycle sitting next to the Christmas tree for me, as I had requested.

Before I could sprint toward the living room, something else purple caught my eye. There they were, sitting on my desk next to my bed, propped up for me to see under my lamp, slightly dimmed: *Prince and the Revolution: Purple Rain* and *Morris Day and the Time: Ice Cream Castle* albums. I silently walked to the albums in excitement, but also with some confusion because I had asked for the *Michael Jackson: BAD* album along with Prince. I figured my mom was really setting the atmosphere for the old "green bracelet" switch from the popular Cosby episode we all loved. Bill Cosby pretends to get the wrong bracelet for his wife, Claire, but as she explains to him that it's the wrong one, he whips out the one she had wanted. I figure the Michael Jackson album is my green bracelet awaiting.

I think I'll outsmart my parents and begin practicing an Oscar-worthy response in my head as I grab the albums and head for the living room. As the only child, the room is filled with gifts for me, a few for my parents, a few for my grandmother, and a rather impressive stack of gifts for Claudine. It looks like there are a few extra in her pile that my parents must've wrapped without me, but my scan of the room was cut short when my dad wheeled a gold and grey ten-speed bike from around the doorway. The bike was not purple, but the letters of my name were carefully placed down the angle bar in purple block letters. I wasn't expecting that, and my response to seeing a bike personalized with my name was not planned, but it was Oscar-worthy.

I danced and ran around the room for a few minutes and was ready to start handing out and receiving more gifts. Halfway through our Christmas festivities, I heard footsteps approach and then banging on our front door. Claudine stood in her pajamas, a glittery Michael Jackson glove on one hand, and three wrapped gifts in the other. We had a short greeting before immediately exchanging gifts.

I smile as Claudine smiles with every gift she opens. I take joy in watching her enjoy a warm Christmas morning in my home, with my parents. It all feels perfect, until I see her pick up a wrapped gift - a big square, the shape of an album. I watch Claudine open the gift. It is an album. *It better not be,* I think. *It is.* All of a sudden, I was witnessing the live Cosby-Claire reaction from my friend, her one hand covered in sparkles, the older holding the Michael Jackson album I dearly coveted. I watched her pink pajama dress fly up and down as she screamed with each jump. Slowly, I turned my head toward my mom to stare her down. *How could she? My Christmas list was clear with correct spelling. And yet, here we are. Claudine with MJ and me with Morris Day.* Mom notices my stare and immediately mouths, "Fix your face." I fix it and quickly wipe away my tears, so I don't get in more trouble.

Claudine grabs the rest of her gifts and runs across the street still screaming to show her mom and younger sisters. Moments after she ran out our door, my mother inquired about what I was thinking. "What's on your mind?" She doesn't ask me how I feel. Mom hardly ever asks about how I feel. It's always about what I am thinking.

"I wanted that album. I thought you knew that. I am your daughter, not Claudine."

My mom doesn't match my emotional intensity. She inquires more about my thoughts, allowing me to explain my beliefs about their decision to give Claudine the MJ album instead of me. The belief that Claudine deserves the album more. The belief that they love her more. The belief that it was impossible for my parents to make this mistake. Both my mother and father spend very little time with my feelings or getting upset about me having these feelings.

Ungrateful and *spoiled* are words never mentioned in this life lesson. My feelings are acknowledged and heard, and then my parents quickly transition into a conversation about my irrational thoughts.

This particular Christmas is so memorable for me not because of the beautiful bike I received or an MJ album that left my house never to return, but because of this roughly fifteen-minute conversation my parents had with me. It is the conversation that will set the groundwork for my understanding of how my parents practice empathy. In this Christmas conversation, my parents never let any heightened emotions take center stage. They are sensitive but metered, and I feel cared for because I feel understood through their interrogation of my thoughts. Sitting in the midst of ripped up wrapping paper and a half-eaten breakfast, my parents connect with me and build a shared understanding that acknowledges and validates my feelings by helping me work through the thoughts and beliefs creating those feelings.

My parents shared stories with me about similar childhood thoughts and experiences they had when they felt their parents' behaviors were unfair or punitive. I have these conversations with my parents a lot as a young girl. They lay a foundation that peaks my awareness and helps me pinpoint which of my thoughts are truthful and which aren't, so that I can better regulate my feelings. They teach me that, in retrospect, I really didn't need an explanation of why I didn't get the album, because when Mom shares that the gift was a strategic plan between the neighborhood moms to ensure Claudine could match a MJ glove with the album, it reminds me to consider the connection of experiences Claudine and I share of not getting what we wanted or asked for. I'm reminded of the many times Claudine did not receive the things she asked for from her mother and the Richardson's. Things in my home that she begged for and never received, including parents that got along. We shared in this experience to different degrees and I had to be reminded of this in a way that investigated my thoughts without chastising me for how I felt. Empathy isn't feeling exactly what another person feels. My parents did not feel the way I felt, yet they showed me understanding and taught me how to do the same.

Empathy is understanding why a person feels the way they do.

Because Empathy is understanding the thoughts and reasoning behind how someone feels, regardless if you agree, and without dismissing or minimizing their feelings in the process, it's impossible for this to be something humans are just born with. There are people who seem to naturally be more concerned for others and more accepting. There are those who are more comfortable and drawn to others' emotions and termed "empath." And yes, I would agree that there are individuals who seem to be more affectionate and naturally sensitive coming out of the womb. But none of those things will automatically lead to the depth of connected understanding that true, lasting empathy provides without modeling. The empathy that we talk about as the prerequisite to compassion and kindness and forgiveness in spite of how we feel must be cultivated.

Empathy is a learned behavior.

The most grossly negligent misconception about empathy is that it is innate. The notion that people either have empathy or they don't is detrimental to our understanding of how empathy should be viewed and employed. Human beings do not come out of the womb with an inherent ability to share understanding, or with a varying ability to connect with things they agree and disagree with.

I have two daughters who are four years apart. When Kayla, my youngest, was three years old, she was much more assertive than my oldest daughter, Aubrey. When Kayla saw a toy or a snack she wanted, she snatched it from her older sister, which would cause Aubrey to cry.

After inquiring about her tears, Aubrey would express to me that her feelings got hurt whenever Kayla ripped possessions from her hands. One afternoon, it was a crunchy Cheeto that Kayla had snatched away. However, replacing the Cheeto back into Aubrey's hands did not stop Aubrey's tears, because she was more disappointed in her sister than she was upset about not having the Cheeto anymore, and she was sad that Kayla would treat her that way. Meanwhile, little three-year-old Kayla just sat there while I consoled Aubrey, staring at us while her little jaws chomped on the Cheeto she'd strategically grabbed when Aubrey's head was turned toward the TV.

In an attempt to teach Kayla a lesson, I snatched the Cheeto out of her hand and ate it (putting Kayla in Aubrey's shoes), but Kayla just laughed hysterically. Both my girls had a different emotional response to the same scenario, because they had contrasting interpretations. As long as there was another Cheeto to be had, Kayla was fine because she knew there were more in the bag. Aubrey was not okay with the unkindness of her sister, regardless if she knew there were more Cheetos in the bag. For Aubrey, it wasn't about the Cheetos. It wasn't about the object. It was about the feeling Kayla's behavior conjured inside Aubrey that upset her. Kayla did not have those same feelings.

On several occasions, I have encountered teachers trying to teach empathy with the "put yourself in their shoes" method, and if the exercise was a flop or the lesson didn't go over well, they deemed those children incapable or not wired for empathy. Children often don't have the same emotional response adults might expect because they don't have the same thoughts driving their emotions. I've worked with many educators who insisted that all of their children should innately connect with their peers' feelings, especially if they have endured similar hardships. But what they get is an older version of the Cheeto scenario and the same frustration I endured, reverting back to the outdated definition of empathy, trying to tap into the empathetic gene by putting my daughter in the shoes of her sister she loves.

We ought to teach our children to listen and validate, like my parents did with me and Claudine, versus the neighbors who were consumed with their own feelings of pity, who rarely listened and remained disconnected. We ought to teach them how to investigate their thoughts, both rational and irrational ones, to better understand why they were feeling a certain way, like my parents did on that Christmas morning. We ought to show them how to connect with similar beliefs, regardless of the particulars, because it's more about the desire to wake up to a Michael Jackson album, or to parents who get along.

If we become dismissive about a child with a seeming inability to connect with other students, we condemn them to be labeled as selfish and unempathetic without investigating their thoughts beneath their behaviors. In this way, we participate in disconnection, we teach children there is something wrong with them if they can't execute the traditional definition of empathy, and we miss an opportunity to model empathy ourselves. Because, ultimately, empathy can't be the actual ability to feel what another person feels, rather it's an investigative effort to understand why a person feels the way they feel.

The Reeducation of Empathy

Relearning our ABCs

My mom and dad taught me that empathy is a skill that must be taught and modeled. The dorms of Kuhlman and Buenger Hall showed me that our outdated concept of empathy creates enmeshed camps of emotionally charged roommates and reactive relationships, and as a result, deters some from pursuing it, even in safe quarters. Olean, NY and the first half of my marriage confirmed for me that equal sacrifice is no replacement for the equal sharing of understanding, but rather a byproduct of empathy. In fact, compassion, forgiveness, patience, along with sacrifice are, to name a few, all byproducts of empathy. And we know this! Why else would we answer all of life's most challenging problems with this famous three-syllable word?

Empathy is printed on hundreds of titles of books and trending on media platforms more and more each day. We understand the power and momentum shift it causes. So why reduce it down to a metaphor about shoes and speak of it as an innate human characteristic that we just do if we care about people? Something as impactful as empathy has to be learned and must come with a clear roadmap on how to practice it. Now is the time to relearn empathy, and just like basic literacy, it starts with our ABCs.

A = Acknowledging Humanity
B = Bypass Your Feeling in Order to Validate Theirs
C = Connect Beliefs

CHAPTER FIVE

Acknowledging Humanity

As simple as this sounds, acknowledging humanity is something that we as a human race have a long history of failing at. And many people continue to fail at this, despite their belief in their own good intentions. Depersonalization and dehumanization, even in its most minute form, executes the opposite sentiment of empathy. Empathy is a connection built through understanding. If we can't first accept our shared humanity, learn to acknowledge our collective faults and misgivings, and embrace one another despite them, understanding and connection will never follow. At best, what follows is tolerance, but tolerance is a form of acceptance that doesn't necessarily require connection.

The dehumanization and devaluation of personhood can happen subtly, yet our concept of it is so narrowed and constrained. Usually, more overt, blatant examples of it, like slavery, are the degree of dehumanization we first think of and recognize. When American history speaks of human beings as property, when we identified men and women as 1/5th a person, we easily recognize these acts of depersonalization. But as we continue the conversation today, addressing the continued denial of equal rights and privilege to certain individuals based on their race, gender, or any other discriminating factor, we diminish that acknowledgement. We fail to collectively value each other as whole people - mind, body, and soul.

Acknowledging humanity means a complete acknowledgement of a person's entire personality, motivations, feelings, intuition, beliefs, and desires; it means acknowledging a whole person in all their gifts and their faults, not just their anatomy. Through

empathy, we acknowledge our shared humanity –
the same feelings we all experience: pain, fear, anger,
excitement, love, joy. It's an acknowledgement that
we both cry. We both dream. We both grieve. We
both desire to care for our children. And when I'm
having a baby as a Black woman, my physical pain
and its emotional expression is real and needs the
same medical attention as other women. My fellow
human beings want to be respected and heard, just
like I do, even if we're different in more tertiary
ways: socio-economic status, religion, political party,
values, intelligence, gender, or nationality. All human
beings have a right to be believed. And if we cannot
acknowledge their humanity by believing their
feelings, their experiences, their stories, there is no
room for connection. You can't understand through
your interpretation or imagination of what it might
be like to fit in their shoes. There are obstacles that
impede this basic acknowledgement of humanity.
The most detrimental is the fear of association.

If the Shoe Fits, Wear it
Fear of Association

"If the shoe fits, wear it." A well-known phrase that means if a description applies to you, then accept it, *own* it. Within this philosophy lays the greatest danger in defining empathy through the metaphor of wearing other people's shoes. Many of us subconsciously define empathy as accepting or wearing a description that applies to someone else as our own. *I know how she feels because I am a slow runner, too. I understand his temper because we are both Geminis.*

Subsequently, we believe if we put ourselves in their shoes then it may appear to others that the shoe fits—that other people will perceive us based on their understanding of another person's beliefs, values, thoughts, behavior patterns, emotions, etc. It's the reason folks who come from different backgrounds, who worship different Gods, who claim different political affiliations have such a hard time even attempting to be empathetic with others who are not the same as them. Our fear of misrepresentation, association with, or acceptance of ideologies we disavow creates a threat. Our fear of association can be too great a burden to bear, so the opportunity for empathy is lost. If we fear that in feeling empathy for a person who is different from us then labels us as the same as them, we cannot create any sense of shared humanity. Our sense of self overrides the moral and ethical imperative we have to empathize with people on the other side of the aisle.

If you have ever been on any kind of social media platform, you are fully aware of the risk involved in showing moral support of any kind. Take a trip down any comments section and you will quickly find them to be mostly judgmental and crass. People often feel nervous to display public support for each other for fear of being associated with another person's values, behaviors, or feelings on a topic. We often think things to ourselves like, *What if the person receiving my support, or even a simple thumbs-up "like" emoji, misinterprets my gesture as acceptance or even a new shared ownership of their situation or problem?* We get distracted from simply being supportive of others by our fear of misperception through association. But there is more on the line than our ambivalence as adults.

Children are not exempt from this fear either. The fear of association phenomenon is even more prevalent in children and adolescents because, as they get older, affiliation or perceived acceptance or rejection from a peer group is a risk they aim to neutralize ASAP. Peer groups are essential in helping shape a child's identity, interests, and self-esteem, and is a necessary part of growth and development. Minimally, the right peer group affords certain luxuries, and the wrong peer group can bring isolation. Because it is a much bigger risk for children and teens to shake up their social structure, they often will not risk it, inhibiting their ability to seize social opportunities to practice and display empathy.

The way we have taught empathy to our children as a form of acceptance by way of the metaphor of walking in someone else's shoes leaves them questioning if being empathetic is worth all the risks that come with being "associated" with another person.

The spring of my sixth grade year I notice my parents behaving strangely. Whispering more than usual, and for a few weeks they seem distant. I'm not sure what is going on, but it seems very important. In fact, it is important and it is life changing. After ten years, I will no longer be an only child. Our family is changed forever. I am stoked about the possibility of having a little sister. In my young mind, I can only imagine what it would be like to have another girl in the home. One to share my room with every day, not just on the weekends with Claudine.

Although my little mind couldn't imagine what a brother would be like, I learned quickly. My little brother Kareem arrives the winter of '87. He is *so* precious and big. And the best part is he does share a room with me for at least a year. I wake him up in the middle of the night while he is sleeping in his crib next to my bed so I can hold him and make him smile. My parents can't figure out why it is so hard to wake us both up in the morning. We don't share a room for long. Immediately after announcing our new family addition, my parents let me know we will have to find a bigger home. I am devastated and I just want to make the house work so I can stay on the street I love and know.

I have a change of heart as we begin looking at homes only a few miles away. Bigger homes with bigger yards that I didn't know we could even afford. It was fun imagining a room with paint colors and furniture I would choose. But as we had to search farther and farther away, the fun wore off. After almost a year of looking, my parents make the decision, without my input, that they will build a home in a developing suburb of West Chester, Ohio. Technically, the suburb was only about a twenty-minute drive away, but it is too far to ride my bike to my friends' houses or to jump on the Metro city bus back and forth.

Our new neighborhood is so much different than Bond Hill. There are no street lights or street signs. My parents get turned around almost each week while visiting the progress of the build. There are no corner stores or Richie's Chicken restaurants in sight. My mother stocks up on ebony-colored stockings at the store near her job in the city so that she doesn't have to make an extra twenty-minute trip for makeup, hair products, or stockings to match her skin tone that she can't find in our new local stores. I am thirteen years old, watching my parents navigate and adjust to our new home and new community.

Summer lazily floated past me while I stayed inside, because when I did venture out, neighborhood boys would call me "nigger." The navigation was much more difficult for me. I never told my parents about it. They were so proud – like ridiculously proud – of the home they built, and I didn't want to ruin that for them. I didn't want to smear their idea of our new home with the racism I was experiencing. As the first day of school approached, I didn't know what to expect. I was hoping to see other girls, but I was curious if the white girls would call me "nigger," too. More than anything, I was hoping to see brown boys and brown girls who looked like me, who would simply call me by name, Jonelle. I think there were just five.

A junior high of three-hundred students had the strangest five Black kids I have ever interacted with in my life. I hadn't even seen these types of Black kids on TV, and there was a good variety on TV in the eighties and early nineties. We had *The Cosby Show,*

What's Happening, Family Matters, Moesha, even the adopted Black kids on *Different Strokes.* But these five Black students in my junior high talked, dressed, and danced so differently than any Black person I had ever been around. Over the course of the year, I concluded that their differences were a result of them either being born in or raised too long in West Chester. They were sweet kids, but I didn't want to be affiliated with them for fear of becoming more like them. In the back of my mind, I recalled something from my aunts and cousins about "not acting white" and "not forgetting where I came from." Point blank, I did not want to be in their shoes, so I did not associate with them.

The irony is I needed them more than they needed me to navigate and adjust to my new normal, yet I kept my distance. I discovered that racist people don't stop being racist to someone because they've known them for a longer time. These five other students were enduring the same struggles I was, for who knows how long, and I had little empathy or understanding for them. We were in the same boat, but I was more concerned about not being associated with them because they cuffed their jeans, listened to

Nirvana, and didn't respond the way I did to being called "nigger." It wasn't as shocking to them as it was to me because they had seemingly built up some immunity toward the word.

As a teenager, I feared the appearance of accepting and owning their culture at the expense of disowning mine. I could have easily related to the other Black kids, but I had zero desire to do so. I could have acknowledged our connection and empathized with them, but I was afraid of losing my identity and becoming associated with labels and other demeaning stereotypes that were passed around – like being called an "Oreo" (black on the outside and white on the inside).

As I reflect on this, it's embarrassing that I rejected them, and I realize how much sharing an empathetic understanding with them could have cultivated the supportive relationships and resilience that I desperately needed. My self-esteem, my ability to adjust to change, and my capacity to develop socially and emotionally as a teenage girl was violently threatened by hateful racism, and I barely survived it because of my fear of losing my identity through being associated with the other Black kids – my criteria for which was superficial, meaningless nonsense that had nothing to do with my character on the inside.

Pride obstructs the pathway toward empathy.

Fear of association is rooted in this all or nothing, stay on one side of the line, black or white thinking. But the truth is in the middle - right smack in the middle of our differences. The truth is we don't have to be all in, and our identity and self-awareness will survive in the middle. It's okay to both agree and disagree with other people, and then to explore the grey area between you.

We are complex, layered beings with the intellectual capacity to dissect the intricacies of our thoughts and emotions, and to do this with and for others is an act of empathy. The grey area is where empathy happens. It's where compromise and unity live, where we can see the humanity of other people more objectively, where we can see not only how we're different but how surprisingly similar we all really are. We need to collectively give ourselves permission to explore different ideas without the tether or burden of association or complete ownership; to praise and encourage curiosity again, so we might combat our stringent thinking and replace it with open-mindedness and understanding.

Fear of association hinders our ability to accomplish the first step of the empathetic process, acknowledging full humanity. Because I didn't want to be associated with the other Black students, I had a hard time acknowledging them as Black students like myself, or acknowledging that we were going through the same experience of racism, regardless of how they talked and what music they listened to.

Fear of association leads to alienation, the antonym of empathy.

CHAPTER SIX

Bypass Your Feelings

to Validate Theirs

Bypassing your feelings in order to validate theirs is the next step in the ABC model. Bypassing how we feel is completely contrary to what most of us believe about empathy. Therefore, it is one of the most difficult things to unlearn. Usually, when most of us (who are not trained in a listening field, like counseling) are listening, we make sure to make eye contact, we participate by engaging body language, like leaning forward and nodding our head, all while trying to figure out what we are going to say and processing how we are feeling. We especially take note of feelings – theirs and our own. And the person who is talking is also anticipating and expecting you to pay close attention to how they feel, and share in that feeling, too.

Having a listener sift through (and not sit in) your emotions is an acquired taste because people typically expect you to share in their feelings in order to exhibit that you care and understand. However, professionals in the listening fields are tasked with doing just that – sifting through and not sitting in other's emotions. Their goal is to establish a rapport through the validation of their client's feelings, and through an expressed understanding of their client without becoming enmeshed. This skill is not limited to trained professionals.

As you recognize your emotions matching theirs, regroup and go back to validating theirs by emphasizing the feelings that they are expressing. Remind yourself that you are the one providing a listening ear of support. Because when both parties are now entangled with emotions, although there is a shared connection, it's not always a lasting one. It's not a lasting connection because feelings are fickle, and the intensity of that shared feeling varies, and feelings are usually temporal. Feeling someone's anger in an attempt to empathize with them may produce a shared connection initially - until one of the individuals has moved on and is no longer mad. And the next time that person wants you to share in their feelings of anger, minimization, or in the dismissal of that feeling is likely to occur because the connection was cut short last time.

Validation is not the collective experience of feeling.

Giving people permission to feel whatever they are feeling because of their human right to do so, regardless if you understand or align with their feelings, is validation. One can validate any feeling that they are not experiencing. Bypassing how you feel will help you validate others, especially when you are feeling completely different about what has happened. Even if the feelings are mutual, the introduction of your own feelings tip the scale and can squeeze out space and attention for validating theirs.

Validation is creating a safe place for connection.

Tipping the Scale
Comparison is the Thief of Empathy

We commonly try to relate to other people's hardship by comparing it to our own. We think that sharing in a person's emotions builds a sense of camaraderie, and to do this, we often liken a person's circumstances to our own experiences, plucking out ones from our lives that we feel are similar. But this tendency overshadows our ability to make true connections, to feel real empathy for a person, and, in turn, truly understand them. When we compare our own experiences to another person's, we tend to conflate how we felt with how we think they should feel, which precludes us from understanding *why* a person actually feels the way they do about a situation. Moreover, comparison is usually provoked and instigated by feelings of regret, jealousy, and disappointment with ourselves. In an effort to mitigate this, we often make a leap into becoming helpers of sorts at this point, telling someone how we were able to successfully navigate a situation similar to theirs. And we do this in the name of inspiring and motivating. But every time you tell someone how you coped with a situation better, how you responded more appropriately, or how you were able to more smoothly endure tougher circumstances, you diminish any sense of a shared understanding you might've had.

Connection, not comparison, leads to inspiration.

When I was tallying how many more sacrifices I'd made versus my husband, I was comparing, or "tipping the scale" – and the focus – towards my feelings and my thoughts, leaving no room for sharing, for empathy, for reconciliation. Tipping the scale of attention towards how much worse, longer, or harder your situation is in comparison to another person's interrupts your ability to actively listen and make space for another person. Realigning the focus on yourself disables you from being able to truly understand the position of the other person. When Bobbi truly let me share during that time of sadness and hopelessness with my daughter, when she listened, absorbed, acknowledged, and validated my feelings, things weren't all going well for her either, yet she never compared her terminal illness to my daughter's diagnosis - a diagnosis categorized and coded as "cosmetic." While it is likely that I will never see my daughter's beautiful thick curls again, the odds are stacked against Bobbi seeing her daughter at all for very much longer. Bobbi still carved out space for me.

It can be hard at times to not monopolize the conversation when you share something in common with someone, especially when you are taking on the emotions of others.

Feelings invite the spirit of comparison because we often express feelings differently.

Feelings are subjective and personal. And actively sifting through a person's feelings to uncover and listen for the beliefs and thoughts behind those feeling requires much more focus and patience while listening to their story than telling your own can provide.

My mom is from eastern Ohio, in the heart of the Appalachian Mountains neighboring West Virginia and Pennsylvania. Her childhood was robbed by poverty, alcoholism, abuse, and domestic violence. At the age of eleven, my grandmother looked my mother in the eyes and told her she couldn't endure the abuse from her husband anymore and that she was leaving, permanently, with only her oldest son, my mom's half brother. In a stupor, my mom stood there with her baby sister on her small, boney hip, surrounded by six other children she now had to help raise.

To do this, my mom often focused on her thoughts. She thought about taking care of herself and siblings. She thought about survival. This specific skill of thinking and remaining thoughtful about her next moves, thoughtful about connections, resources, family, and how to cope with Appalachian poverty ironically groomed her to be the most empathetic person I've ever known. It's almost hard to comprehend – *How can my mother show such compassion and understanding toward people who were cruel to her?* But more than that, I would come to wonder how my mother became so adept at expressing empathy for people with problems that paled in comparison to her own experience. If a person complained to my mom but they had running water and electricity at home, I found myself resenting their feelings, thinking to myself, *You're fine! My mother had nothing!* Nonetheless, Mom always encouraged others, never saying things like, "If I can do it with the little I had then surely you can make it in your situation." Instead, Mom was thoughtful, and related to others without minimizing their experience; connected with them without judging them. Mom did the work necessary to truly access and practice empathy.

My sweet mother keeps on the shoes she walked through a traumatic childhood with. Yet she easily connects with people in solidarity by connecting their thoughts with hers. I think if she allowed her emotions and the feelings surrounding her childhood to get involved while making a connection with another person, she would run the risk of comparing her pain to theirs.

Empathy was also the tool that helped her succeed in her career. As director at the social security office, my mother's extraordinary ability to empathize with the public she served and the employees she managed visibly stood out. Because of her, it became a healthy working environment that had previously been a stressful one because of the poverty, mental illness, and desperation of people in need that they were serving. She created a culture of empathy and connection with her staff and modeled as much as she served the public. And this all happened without any paid consultant coming in to teach about work culture and making your employees feel valued.

I remember when my mom decided to attend night school in order to learn sign language. She felt like her connection to deaf clients was lessened when she had to rely on an interpreter. Every time I spoke with my mom, up until the day of her retirement, she was always baking an employee a cake. She knew so much about her employees' individual lives. Even the employees she had to let go. "Mom, what's the occasion this time?" I asked on our weekly phone calls. A birthday, a car loan paid off, an employee's daughter making the honor roll, a dog died, a celebration, a victory, a defeat, a rough week survived. My mom has plenty of thoughts and experiences when it comes to trials and overcoming them, defeats and small victories, and especially survival; she can connect with successes and survival, no matter the scale, and then she celebrates it with a double chocolate three-layer cake.

But there were moments when fatigue set in for my mom and dad while raising a second child at forty years old. Not only is patience and stamina necessary to validate feelings without tipping the scale, it is also needed to resist simply creating your own story for someone's else's life as a ready-made blueprint. Take my younger brother for example. My parents have their own blueprint in mind for Kareem to follow in lieu of hearing and understanding his journey. The blueprint is based on a set parenting style. Kareem is quite different than their first born. He is way more active with a shorter attention span than I had as a child. And my parents are less active a decade older in raising him, too. They go from watching their little seven-year-old girl listen to the coach and follow instructions and game schemes, resulting in scored goals on the soccer field, to watching my seven-year-old brother struggle to stay focused on the coach's instructions, playing in the dirt while his peers run around him to score.

Although Kareem severely struggles to focus his attention on sports and school, he is brilliant. He loves to read and takes pride in his extensive vocabulary. He picks up concepts quicker than most, and I still call him when I don't understand a complex trending concept or anything technology related. He uses his large vocabulary in extensive drawn out conversations with my tired parents. I was out of the house by the time he turned ten, but I know my parents implemented the same parenting model with my brother as they did with me. *You stay active, you stay involved, you stay consistent, and most importantly, you stay in the books.* This model needed tweaking for Kareem, but I suspect my parents were too tired and less patient to explore or hear out anything too different than the story and blueprint they had created for him.

There are moments when I see my parents feel frustrated with Kareem, as they spend little time validating his feelings and understanding his thoughts. Kareem has a lot of thoughts. Philosophical thoughts about the world, human nature, and ideals. I remember my mom and dad entertaining these thoughts and beliefs less than they did mine as a child, and spent more time expressing their disinterest in my brother's sharing of his feelings, and more interest in improved results – better grades, a cleaner room, more responsible decision making. Kareem, like other young men, experiences this absence of validation, especially in the absence of unmet expectations. We chalk it up to stereotypical masculine norms of toughness to succeed in spite of your emotional compass. Society tells Kareem to *suck it up*, to *not cry* about his feelings, and to *tough it out.* Society tells Kareem he'll be fine, and he will have to be strong to survive. My father reminds him that the real world doesn't care about how he feels, especially being a young African-American male. He shouldn't expect the world to acknowledge his humanity.

Culturally, females are more commonly encouraged to share their feelings. They are also more commonly expected to operate out of emotion, and in this way, we've tipped the scales against our men and their ability to connect with and validate feelings. We don't do it for them, so they can't later model it for us. We need to recognize and acknowledge that men feel the same emotions as women – anger, excitement, disappointment, fear, indecision, depression, joy – and stop expecting them to suppress certain feelings, to just perform, while overestimating others. Remember, A is for acknowledgment, acknowledging humanity in its complete fullness: mind, body and soul. Not only are we excluding men from the full expression of their own human emotions, we are disallowing them from participating in fully embodied, empathetic relationships with other people.

Teenage boys feel insecure, confused, impressionable, and moody, just like my thirteen-year-old daughter does now. And sometimes, males like my brother experience all of these feelings more often and more deeply than their sisters. But we often tip our expectations and disregard the emotions in our boys we don't want to see – effectively crowding them out – while embracing, and expecting, the emotional hurricane that it is believed to be a teenage girl. This leaves girls feeling overwhelmed, boys feeling neglected, and both disconnected through comparison without the tools it takes to build a bridge between themselves with empathy.

When a girl cries, we compare her to all girls. We say things like *it's not that big of a deal* and *she cries about everything.* If a boy cries, we call him *different* and *sensitive.* We emasculate him for his expression by comparing him to our cultural ideal of how a boy should operate, and then criticize the boy when he becomes a man who doesn't express his feelings in a way that suggests he feels the way we feel.

It was year five of my marriage when I really came to terms completely with the fact that if I didn't find a way to be more connected and understanding, less dismissive of my husband's feelings, and stop tipping the scale of how much worse I had it, we weren't going to make it. My jealousy of his career and his pursuit of professional goals constantly landed me on my knees in prayer. All of the advice I received from my friends, pastors and parents, although well intended, led me back to my knees, to my pleading, asking God for answers that would save my marriage.

Ultimately, the answers did come. The circumstances forced me to deeply re-evaluate my approach to marriage, and the expectation of my husband to mutually sacrifice and suffer. The real work of empathy begins here for the both of us. This is when I reflected on all the times I'd spent tipping the scale, on comparing what I thought I deserved to what I had and he had, never taking the time to be present and grateful for what WE had. I reflected on my pride, my ego, and the excuses I'd made to myself for not fulfilling my purpose. And Jeff joined me in self-reflection of his own. To learn empathy, I had to unlearn the story I was telling myself about what empathy really is and how it could or could not help my marriage.

Comparison confiscates permission to be heard and understood.

The one thing that has been evident to me is that being in moments of comparison rather than connection is a very dark place filled with loneliness.

Allowing envy to interfere and block your opportunities to validate, improve, encourage, uplift, celebrate, and relate to someone else is such a dark place to be. Humans are relational beings that need each other for physical and emotional survival. Authentic connection generates the support and stability we need to navigate life and the trials that accompany it. No one who has ever been successful in their profession, or impactful on others, or has experienced joy, peace, or love without being connected or understood by another human being. If empathy is the catalyst for all of this, then why in the world do we struggle with it? We struggle because we get in our own way. Our own ambitions, our emotional instability, our lack of self-awareness, the way we compare and covet what others have perpetuates our struggle.

My loss is GREATER than yours.
You have MORE control over your situation than I did.
I had LESS help.
They had to endure this LONGER than you.
You don't matter more than I matter.

Envy and comparison is a byproduct of disconnection.

CHAPTER SEVEN

Connect Beliefs

Why people feel the way they do comes from the beliefs they carry behind their feelings. Connecting with a person's beliefs instead of the feelings they express helps you create a more authentic connection that is supportive because it is empathetic. Our feelings can be poor indicators of the problems we need to face, which are most commonly the product of thoughts. Feelings take our breath away, cause butterflies in our stomachs, and goosebumps on our arms. They are powerful manipulators and triggers for many behaviors. Feelings are subjective and often reactive, yet they are important because they leave clues that can reveal and uncover our thoughts and beliefs. That's why it is so important to validate feelings, creating a safe space for people to further talk and unearth the beliefs they're holding underneath their feelings.

The traditional understanding of empathy creates disconnection between students and childhood peers as well, precluding them from fully being able to understand the emotional consequences of their actions and developing a more intricate understanding about the ways humans are connected to one another. For example, if Cole is upset because Jack told their peers an embarrassing rumor about Cole, their teacher might reprimand Jack by saying something like, "Put yourself in his shoes. Wouldn't you be upset if someone said that about you?" But Jack comes from a large family and has three older brothers who regularly tease him. He has no frame of reference or context for why Cole is upset. He can't put himself in Cole's shoes because he doesn't think he has any lived experience to inform him of what it might be like to be Cole.

Jack rebuffs, "Nope, I would think it was funny. We clown each other all the time at my house. I'm just playing. Y'all take things too seriously." Jack doesn't think Cole is justified in feeling upset or embarrassed. He doesn't view Cole's feelings and upset as warranted. Where do we go from here? How can we teach and encourage empathy if our expectation of Jack here is to develop a new understanding from thin air? In a way, our traditional understanding of empathy asks that we be able to preempt each other's feelings, and this is an unrealistic ask of anyone, let alone of children who are still emotionally and psychologically developing.

What if teachers led with calling out thoughts and experiences instead? What if we didn't impose an expectation on children to feel one another's feelings, or to preempt each other's reactions? Perhaps the adult in this situation might respond differently: "I bet you Cole is upset because he doesn't believe he deserved to be disrespected. Have you ever been disrespected? Or have you ever thought you had been disrespected?" With this response, the adult is asking Jack to stay in his own shoes – to access his own experiences and his thoughts around them as a way to empathize with Cole.

This method also opens a doorway for dialogue between the adult and Jack. It isn't accusatory, rather it asks Jack to participate in the lesson itself. Through more exploration, the adult in this situation has an opportunity to show Jack that he and Cole have both shared the belief of being disrespected, even if the circumstances were different. All situations are bound to be different, and how we feel about things – even how we show our feelings – are also very different, so telling someone they should be able to channel the same feelings as another person is a doomed conquest. Instead, we need to validate feelings, no matter what they are. The adult in this conversation has an opportunity to validate a time when Jack felt disrespected and then connect that to Cole's current feelings, giving Jack the opportunity to validate Cole's feelings and understand better why Cole is upset.

Beyond this interaction between the two boys is a learning opportunity for the rest of their class. A script for the teacher might sound something like this:

"Class, let's talk about disrespect for a minute. I'm curious to know what sort of behaviors you believe to be disrespectful, and I'm going to write them on the board. Some may agree or disagree with the examples of disrespect we put on the board, but we are all talking about how disrespect looks to each of us. Next, we can talk about how we all feel when we think we are being disrespected. The feelings may vary in degree, but they will likely be similar – angry, sad, hurt, betrayed, and so on. Class, it's important for us to realize that underneath the varying emotions we share here, and the different acts of disrespect we identify, we are still talking about a common belief all of us have, which is that we deserve respect."

Empathy uncovers the common shared beliefs underneath varying emotions and reactions.

There is Safety in Your Thoughts
The Games We Play

To keep yourself in your own shoes while connecting with another person's beliefs, you can ask yourself the question, *Have I ever...?* Ask yourself if you've ever thought or believed in the same things as another person, regardless of the specific details of the experience or your feelings. When you can match your same beliefs and thoughts with others, all the while keeping your feelings in your own shoes about those beliefs to better understand another person's, you connect with them in a pure and meaningful way.

During my junior year in college, I was finally introduced to a drinking game called *Never Have I Ever*, also known as *Questions*. Nearly every waking hour of my college career is spent in a basketball gym, on the road with my team, or serving in my sorority's chapter, so the opportunity to simply unwind and just be in the moment during my downtime is seldom. Once I get a chance to engage, I notice how everyone is simply carefree, playing the game. It is second nature to them. They obviously have three more years of experience than I do.

As we play, I'm thinking about trust – the trust people have of one another, about the atmosphere of safety in the room, preparing us for the full in-depth confessions this game will spark. I think more about distrust and about the risk of me not being able to get back to Xavier's campus. And I also think about the prophetic nature of the game that hooks people up later on that night. I rarely play this game on my small campus. Instead, I venture over near the University of Cincinnati. I'm afraid someone will breach the rules of confidentiality that come with this game, and I think about backing out while our cups are being filled.

Sitting in an off-campus apartment with my fellow sorority sisters and future forever friends, red cups in hand, I am apprehensive about playing for fear of being labeled as *lame*. Every time a person in the group reveals they've never done something (usually provocative or taboo), everyone who has done this thing has to drink up. This act of raising the red cup is a public confession, and we sit around the room in a moment of silence each time, reacting to what others admit to having done.

I am in awe of how safe people feel raising that red cup to their lips. Fortunately, for me, it is a pretty sober game. Turns out, up until this point, I've never done a lot of things. But this doesn't mean I am not extremely nervous to play. I worry about someone cleverly figuring out how to uncover more of me and my fantasies. I pray that no one gathered around me with Vodka filled to the brim in their red cup recognizes thoughts as behaviors. I've never done a lot of things, but I've certainly THOUGHT about doing a lot of things! *Never Have I Ever (Thought About)* would have my business all on Short Vine Avenue, and me drunk like a skunk.

Never Have I Ever is a game of shared connection via experiences. It is a game of validation and safety. The mutual act of sharing creates a safe place of vulnerability with tons of permission for you to admit to any- and everything. Even if you are the only one who raises your red cup, you're unlikely to face any harsh judgment. When only one person raises their cup, everyone else usually becomes suspicious of each other instead. On rare occasions, there are a few stray side-eyes that are always quickly dismissed, left without judgement.

The game created a special sentiment that permeated the room and assured us we are more the same than we are different. The game proved that we shared similar experiences that created a bonding of connection. A connection that still respected differences in the midst of strong variations of feelings expressed throughout the proposed scenarios unveiled. Imagine how deeper the connection and common understanding would have been if shared thoughts were explored no matter the details of the situation. The miseducation of empathy his fallen short by not pursuing this step of connecting shared beliefs as fellow human beings. Our current notion has loosely explored acknowledging humanity and believing someone's story and then relied on us to fill in the rest by just being empathetic. This is the step that seals the deal of understanding. Asking yourself have you ever thought similarly in any type of situation. Have you ever thought...

This is hard.
I regret the decision I made
I want to start over.
I need more.

Remember, thoughts generalize across human experience and human reactions, unlike feelings, which are subjective, personal, and at times difficult to accurately describe.

I want my family to be safe.
It is out of my control.
I need help.
This is unfair.
I am afraid.
I want more.
I've never been in this position before.

These are examples of thoughts that are shared among all types of people but across different situations and circumstances. Regardless of what feelings these thoughts produce in different people, we can relate to one another through an understanding of the thoughts surrounding or fueling any emotion.

CHAPTER EIGHT

Archetypes of Empathy

I value and understand empathy more and more as I reflect on my life and my relationships. Not the miseducation of empathy. Not the imposter that causes me to feel confused with sympathy, overwhelmed with trying to feel what others are feeling, frustrated with sacrifice, distracted with comparisons, and leaves me doubtful about my ability to connect on a deeper level. The ABC steps of empathy (Acknowledging humanity, Bypassing your feelings to validate theirs, and Connecting with shared beliefs to facilitate understanding) has shined through and manifested itself in characters or expressions of empathy. And unfortunately, other characters pretending to be empathy, are falling short of the ABC steps. I have either been or seen all of these characters.

THE CHEERLEADER

For over thirty years, I have sat in stadium seats, half paying attention to the cheerleaders back flipping on the sidelines. Cincinnati Bengals and Reds games and University of Cincinnati and Xavier basketball games were a special part of my childhood. My mother loves sports, and I can remember, as early as age six, jumping off the porch and heading down the street, leaving my dad behind, waving through the screen door, walking to the Cincinnati Gardens to watch college basketball, a few blocks away from my childhood home.

Unlike basketball games during the crisp winter, my dad didn't miss many Cincinnati Reds baseball or fall Bengal football games. Not because he loves football and baseball but because he loves the beautiful summer and fall nights, a bag of peanuts and a cold beer, and a good read. He keeps an Isaac Asimov book with him, folded in his back pocket. My dad doesn't go to games to cheer on the athletes, and I don't go to see the cheerleaders. The smiling women dressed in short skirts and firmly gripping pom-poms only intrigue me when they carry on, hooting and hollering, all while their poor Bengals are down by thirty. Similarly, I watch the UC college basketball cheerleaders still look to their fellow disappointed Bearcat fans, consistently cheering, while the Crosstown Shootout trophy and year-long bragging rights are way out of their reach. I watch, impressed, as the cheerleaders continue to jump, smile, and chant, even if all they have left to celebrate is one or two more good plays.

A cheerleader's job is to be positive, enthusiastic and supportive, regardless of what's happening or what they expect to happen. I can identify with this because I've witnessed their power of momentum. Over and over again, as young as six years old, I watch the cheerleaders and the fans pull their team out of a deficit with consistent praise. The crowd gets louder and louder with each basket made or first down gained. That vocal affirmation transforms one or two good plays into five or six. Cheerleaders shift the momentum of many games, all the time. They motivate the fans, who in turn motivate the behaviors of the players. They have the power to change the atmosphere and create shifts in the confidence and swagger of a team – shifts that have the potential to change the final outcome of the game. And that's why they keep cheering. And that's why this expression of attempted connection and empathy is so popular.

Today's society is inundated with self-help books, podcasts, and life coaches, proving that humanity is looking to feel better, be affirmed, and be motivated to change their situation towards victory. People want help with improving how they feel and changing how they think. No matter how small or big the victory is, there is a cultural push for us to be connected to winning, packaged in a one size fits all formula, no matter the timing or our readiness. Just do it! And start now! Change your mindset! Change your thoughts! Wake up early! Write down your goals! Make a vision board and execute! Although encouraging and inspiring, the cheering loses its understanding and empathetic soul. Where is the validation of how you're feeling? Where is the connection to where you are in your journey and readiness to be motivated? There are plenty of moments in our lives, due to the time and situation, when we are not understood and connected to a cheerleader whose sole attention and focus is on winning.

Cheerleaders cheer regardless of whether their team is winning or losing.

"She will be fine."
"She is still beautiful."
"Look on the bright side - it's just hair and nothing too life threatening."

This is what the cheerleaders in my life told me in an effort to be empathetic toward Kayla's alopecia diagnosis. The cheerleaders in my life encouraged me to move past sadness and my defeated attitude.

They insisted I look on the bright side and see the glass half full. They love me, had great intentions, and really wanted to see me win and smile again. Their keen focus was on motivating me one play at a time. But this persistence, cheering me on no matter what the scoreboard forecasted for Kayla, often felt like minimization, lackluster validation, and selective listening.

The Cheerleader's consistent positivity minimized the deficit and the loss I was struggling with, as well as minimized my feelings in an effort to shift my concentration towards the possibility of things getting better. Ultimately, regardless of their intentions, that felt dismissive. They waited, with their ears only tuned in to cheer, hoping I might find some hope somewhere through their cheers and join them. But I didn't feel heard or validated and that made me feel weak—because now I'm questioning whether or not my feelings of sadness and defeat are even appropriate. *Do I lack faith? Do I lack gratitude for the diagnosis not being more debilitating?* When I try to express my thoughts and feelings out loud, they're interrupted with The Cheerleader's favorite chant:

"But…"

"Girl, BUT you got this."
"BUT you are strong, and I know you will get through this."
"BUT if anybody can get through this, it's you."
"BUT we serve a God that is able."

BUT your timing is off! There is a time for motivation, but that time can only come after a person feels acknowledged and validated through an established connection.

I needed to feel heard before I could think about feeling motivated. I needed step A. Acknowledgement that human beings grieve loss regardless of the type. I needed step B. Permission to feel sad, guilty, fearful for my daughter's future. I needed C. Connection of shared beliefs to eliminate the feelings of immense loneliness on an island of not knowing any other parent of an alopecian. I wasn't in any condition to play. I was not healthy enough to play, let alone win. The Cheerleader's mission is to change the atmosphere of a game regardless of the score and health of the players. They keep trying to uplift the mood, and remain optimistic until the last whistle is blown and the game is over. Although they're loving people who are full of good intentions, this is problematic.

Empathy doesn't require a change in mood.

The cheerleaders around me were trying to pull me away from conflict instead of helping me confront it, so their caring efforts didn't feel helpful. Yet. There is a mood and atmosphere more conducive to The Cheerleader and the way they express empathy. And it's when the shock and disbelief wear off, when people begin to feel glimpses of control over their lives again, once a person's emotions are no longer overwhelming and consuming – when it's not a series of losses or a losing season anymore – not before. The Cheerleader is the person who can share in your newfound perspective, who can help you see joy where you once couldn't, but they can't help you face the hard stuff first, so while they cheer through loss after loss, it can leave you feeling small and insecure.

After three years of marriage and moving to New York, my mother morphed into my cheerleader after empathy was established by a more impactful character of empathy. Because she had been married for twenty-five years, she knew when it was time to start rooting me on and grabbing hold of those one or two "positive" plays. If she had tried to be my cheerleader during that first year in New York, in a darker time when I felt like I was losing everything – my career, my home, my sense of identity – our mother-daughter relationship would have suffered. In this way, I lost valuable years with some cheerleading friends who looked at me while I excavated the turmoil in my marriage, and then said things like, "But you and Jeff love each other," or, "But at least you have a man who provides and who adores you," and, "But you understand the game and coaching lifestyle more than most, because you played."

Juxtaposed to this, and in all of my mother's divine wisdom, she waited to (sparingly) use "but." Because of this, our relationship grew. She had perfect timing, and she didn't ask me to see the hopeful possibilities until she made sure my thoughts and feelings about how hard things felt were heard. With every cheer of encouragement, my mother reminds me of my resilience, points out what I have control over, reveals the small wins in my marriage and being a first-time mom. At the right time, cheerleaders can create strong connections, shift mindsets, and motivate beliefs. They can be the most useful companion once your journey has moved out of the shock, disbelief, or strong feelings, and into a place of renewal.

THE BLANKET

The Blanket is a character of connection who excels in listening and validation. When I think of a Blanket, I think of my Grandmother Selena. She is my father's mom, standing close to six feet tall, usually wearing sizable heels, Mary Kay makeup, and a fashionable scarf meticulously tied around her neck. Even though she isn't the grandmother type you imagine rocking back and forth in a wooden chair with a blanket draped over her, I still think of her when I hear the word "blanket."

Like clockwork every holiday gathering, Grandmother Selena baked several sweet potato pies, a huge dish of macaroni and cheese, and dished out packed samples of Mary Kay beauty products to the women and little girls. After a few hours of festivities, Grandmother Selena wraps a blanket over her and settles restfully into a chair. It doesn't matter which chair she is sitting in – all she needs is a warm blanket to put herself asleep. She tucks it close to her shoulders and neck and instantly her head begins to tilt forward. In the midst of children running around the house, the TV blasting, and a Spades game at the kitchen table, Grandmother Selena rests peacefully.

The warmth and comfort of the blanket puts my grandmother to sleep and grants her peace in the midst of noise. In the same manner, The Blanket character of empathy has the potential to do the same. Many of us have friends, family, mentors, and even trusted colleagues who we call on for this type of comfort and validation. They lay their attention and intentional presence on us. They listen for every opportunity to give you permission for you to be you; permission to express the good, the bad, and the ugly without judgement. Blankets provide a safe place for self-examination because they are really, really patient listeners. They sit in the power of silence when someone is repeating the same part of their story over and over again. Oftentimes, when people are in disbelief, they ruminate and repeat themselves in an effort to process their thoughts and come to grips with the unexpected. Blankets offer a very useful and supportive expression of empathy during these times. Their impressive patience allows time for people to process feelings of grief, sadness, shock, and frustration.

Empathy requires patience to form shared understanding.

The last thing I needed when my daughter was diagnosed with alopecia was someone impatiently cheering me on toward feeling better. I needed the comfort of a patient listening ear and the sweet and easy presence of someone hearing me, giving me permission to feel any way I needed to – guilty, sad, angry, confused. I needed my church friends to pray for me and my daughter without expressing to me a promised "winning" healing on the way with visible excitement of faith. I needed my friends who were just as sad as I was to be confident in their ability to balance their tears and sadness for me with their validating words. I believed most of them felt that they would be too emotional and too heavy of a blanket. But their tears would have validated mine, yet their sobbing would have made me feel worse. Blankets have the tricky task of perfecting a balance of temperature. Although my pride and need for control would disagree, I desperately needed a blanket to cover me while I sat still, so I could find peace in the process. I didn't want to admit that I needed covering, for fear of being consumed by the heaviness of other's emotions too - the weight of their blanket.

Some blankets are hot, heavy, and weigh too much. The Blanket's emotions have the potential to be more intense than yours. Think of that one loyal person, your ride or die, who loves you unconditionally, but who is prone to getting so involved in supporting you that they may end up needing the same support. The weight of their feelings now enmeshed with yours is smothering. My husband can be smothering in this way. When I get really upset about work, or friends, or nearly anything, I reluctantly look to gain support from my husband. Jeff is a Blanket, especially when I express anger. He gets easily fired up when I'm mad, so by the time I'm done venting, I have to calm him down! In doing this, I then find myself minimizing my own feelings and experiences just to reduce his reaction. "No, I'm not that mad. I'm just annoyed."

Blankets create such a safe place for feelings that they are tempted to join in with their own, ironically making it possibly a less safe place to share. Because they lovingly invest an incredible amount of effort in imagining how you feel, consequently, they've convinced themselves that they feel the same way. In an attempt to empathize and connect, The Blanket thinks back to personal experiences that caused them to feel the same way you currently do. Their emotions are also present, with the potential of jumping in the other person's shoes, jeopardizing and possibly monopolizing the connection. Some people don't have to think back to a time they felt the same. They immediately react to your emotions, especially when they care so much about you. Instead of carefully sharing validations, shared experiences, and thoughts back and forth, like Bobbi and I shared over wine and chocolate, the conversation risks becoming an emotional tug of war that begins to confuse and muddle your original feelings. People like my mom and Grandmother Selena, though, have this unique way of leaving their shoes on in order to allow me to walk in mine. They are Blankets with emotional boundaries set in place to support others in their time of need without focusing on themselves and their emotions.

Wisdom lightens the weight of your blanket.

As a child, there was only one woman who didn't cry in front of me when they saw my discolored face. One. My Grandmother Selena! My grandmother cries all the time, though mostly tears of joy and gratitude. She cries at church while praising God. She cries at the kitchen table as she expresses her love and admiration for my father, her eldest son. She cries at graduations and Christmas dinners. She cries while watching Oprah give away cars. But she did not cry around me when everyone else did. Instead, she approached me with thoughtful presence and empathy. She thought about what I needed without indulging her own feelings. She is always present, listening with her shoes on her feet.

And she continued to be my blanket in college. Grandmother Selena's home on Kenny Avenue is a mile away from Xavier University, and when I am consumed with feeling less than about my basketball abilities, or not connecting with other girls on campus, or experiencing another fight with a new boyfriend, I call her up and ask to come visit. She always says yes, even if she has to reschedule a Mary Kay consultation. She welcomes me into her home with a big hug and lets me know that there is food on the stove. She speaks about the food like she didn't just whip it up for me when I called. But I knew by her insistence that I should give her an hour or so to straighten up, that she needs time to actually cook me one of my favorite dishes. (The house looks the same every time I visit - pink Mary Kay order slips everywhere.) She is consistent and loving and considerate of my needs.

My grandmother is a thin blanket, like the one she wraps herself in right before dozing off. She is warm. She is comforting. She is mindfully present. But she doesn't allow my emotions to trigger hers. I am the granddaughter she is extremely proud of. I am the granddaughter all of her church friends know about. I am the granddaughter of the son who she proudly cries about. It's not that she is not invested in how I feel. It's not that she's not listening and responding to my complaints for hours and hours before I begrudgingly return to campus. Remember, it's not that she is not an emotional person. She is! She just understands how to strategically place herself on me without giving me any added weight that makes it too warm or too heavy.

Blankets are an intimate expression of empathy that provide unbelievable connected understanding when expressed at the right temperature. However, it is a tricky expression that asks you to balance your own emotional boundaries within an established relationship. Established relationships provide the safety and comfortability required for Blankets to lay on the concerns being shared. Very rarely are Blankets an effective expression of empathy within relationships that are fairly new or surfaced. Relationships in work settings, and other non-intimate places just doesn't leave a lot of room for Blankets to make a connection. Remember with this expression, connection and shared understanding is cultivated through a patient listening ear and the validation of feelings. Because of the time needed for Blankets to connect, they are more conducive in certain arenas that allow for this time and intimacy. The limitation will always be that the effectiveness of Blankets is highly dependent on an established rapport and/or the comfortability of both parties, an appropriate and conducive setting combined with a good sense of timing, and steady temperature of the Blanket's own emotional boundaries.

THE OPERATOR

How may I direct your call?

In a world of technology, I breathe a sigh of relief when I actually hear a live voice answer with these six words: "How may I direct your call?" No computer on the other end, programmed to hear keywords in your answer that lead to the next series of questions, which then leads to another computerized response question that may or may not lead to a live person in the correct department to help you with your specific need. When I get a live human operator, I feel more confident in getting the specific help that I need because of the opportunity to be understood through my explanation of exactly what I am looking for. I can explain in more detail what I've already tried, who I have been directed to before but was unable to help me, and who should actually be able to assist. An automatic system doesn't have the depth of capabilities of a listening operator.

To empathize is to act.

The act of empathy can include vocal encouragement (The Cheerleader), active listening (The Blanket), and finding resources (The Operator). I have close friends who are Operators. They gravitate towards trying to find something or someone that might help the situation as they have a knack for being resourceful. As connectors, they match people and resources when things are going well and when they are not. Although I, too, am inspired by my mother's childhood story of survival, and carry a desire to help others through action, I also find myself to be an Operator. But I am reminded of The Operator's limitations when I act out this expression of empathy.

When Operators are in action mode, they are listening for problems they can find resources for. They are not listening to be a support or to validate feelings. They are operating out of an authentic purpose of servitude. There are Operators who work for church ministries and who volunteer for organizations. Unfortunately, at times, service and mission work is being done without true connection although their authentic intention is to care for others. Because Operators are helpers, they find ways to be efficient enough to help as many individuals as possible by maximizing their time in sourcing out help. Also, Operators are sometimes birthed out of sympathy. Feeling sorry for someone motivates Operators to find a solution to relieve the discomfort or sorrow of both others and themselves. *How can I, with access to resources, direct your call, you poor thing I feel sorry for?* Helping or directing a call (or need) to a third party, service, or resource is a byproduct of empathy, but cannot work in lieu of.

Helping others without connecting and understanding others is not empathy. It is charity.

In between the unimaginable neglect and abuse my mother experienced, tucked away in the mountains, under the thumb of a drunk coal miner father, are moments of relief and hope. There are people who step up to try and help my mom; Operators expressing empathy the only way they know how to. There's a grade school teacher, a religious woman, who teaches in a one-room segregated school on the hill called "Brown School." My mother loves her teacher and the safety she provides during the school day. The teacher doesn't talk to my mom much about home life, but tries to provide services, food, and positive outlets for my mom and her siblings. There are also aunts and other visiting relatives who do the same for my mother during her school years.

Aunt Harriet, my grandfather's baby sister, doesn't entertain conversations with my mom about her brother's alcoholism, violence, nor the neglect of his children. She comes periodically with hugs, clothes, and money. Aunt Harriet provides for my mother off and on until graduation, meeting her eyes with sympathy, but never expressing it out loud. On my mother's graduation day, her aunt slips her bus fare and tells her to hide it, to pack her things to come live with her in Pittsburgh so she can attend the University of Pittsburgh.

"Don't tell anyone. Just leave." My aunt arranges for housing with a family member and a job at the hospital where she works as a registered nurse. My mother often refers to my Aunt Harriet as the one who saved her life, who "removed me from the hell I was living in."

Operators can be lifesavers.

We need Operators when we don't have the means or emotional stability to acquire resources for ourselves. Emotions can cloud judgement and interrupt clear thinking. Operators help us think things through, or they find someone to help us think things through. They not only connect us to resources and people, but they also connect us to well thought-out solutions and a sense of clarity. They draw from their own experiences and the resources which helped them, but they are also interested in helping find new resources that might better suit your needs. They are very solution-focused, and proper solutions require some degree of objectivity, which can ironically present as less empathetic.

Operators might limit the time they spend listening to feelings and validating them, making them less impactful on people who need to be heard – who aren't ready for advice or an action plan yet. In these cases, when a person who is still in the throes of grief or sadness turns to The Operator for help, they can feel passed off or disregarded. The Operator simply doesn't have a patient listening ear that can help you parse out your feelings. They'd rather help you solve the root problem. In this way, my mother appreciated and valued my aunt "directing" her young adult life out of the mountains, but as a young girl with no mother, she could've used someone present – something more than clothes and soap.

The academic advisors and faculty members who I confided in during my first few years adjusting to college were Operators. When I complained about basketball, they simply directed me towards financial aid and other avenues to help assist me in paying for my schooling rather than relying on my scholarship money. They didn't spend time sifting through my feelings about my insecurities, loneliness, and doubt adjusting to new roles and new expectations.

Sifting is examining thoroughly in order to isolate that which is most important or useful. Sifting is empathy.

Operators are connectors, but they bring resources and actionable assistance that overshadows an interpersonal connection through sifting that is emotionally comforting. The Operator can provide you with tangible support and physical connections that can help lead you more safely down a new or uncertain path, and this is something we all need at times. The Operator minimizes themselves, outside of what they can do, as the thing that's needed, often precluding them from being patient or present for you, rather they are prepared to outsource your needs appropriately. They pass over what is needed first: connection. Operators assume that you want help solving a problem rather than processing it.

Understanding doesn't mean solving.

Similar to Blankets and Cheerleaders, there is a time and place when Operators of empathy are most effective. Yet the expression of each of these three are incomplete by themselves. Operators don't consider the ABCs of practicing empathy. They don't fully acknowledge the person's need for a cathartic emotional release, for psychological processing, and human connection. They do not bypass their feelings to solve the problem, nor do they bypass their feelings of uneasiness with unresolved problems, conflicts, or others' distress in front of them. And lastly, instead of participating in C, connecting themselves to shared beliefs, they outsource and connect you with resources. It's very frustrating practicing empathy as an Operator because you really desire to help others but because the ABC model is not activated, all of your efforts are likely received as charity assignments.

THE FIXER-UPPER

The Fixer-Upper is the automated computer operator – the programmed system that selectively listens for keywords to provide a quick answer that might apply. It is not the live operator who is trying to listen to solve the specific problem. The Fixer-Upper is not even interested in hearing the details of the problem in order to find the best fitting solution. They are impatient, poor listeners, and often act in this role in order to avoid having to be empathetic. The Fixer-Upper would rather find a broad solution and quick fix that might apply. There is no time to establish rapport, trust, or to discover a safe place to intervene. They are uncomfortable and sometimes even annoyed by your need for understanding. I've introduced The Fixer-Upper as an expression of empathy because it is an imposter of empathy, often mislabeled and disguised as empathy.

As a coach's wife for many years, I've listened to wives, and myself, express disconnect with their husband, not because of the amount of time they spend on the road but from lack of understanding and validation. Oftentimes, our husbands' response has been to hurry up and fix the problem in order to avoid the time needed to understand it. Maybe because of the pressures and demands of their work, they are tired and overwhelmed from investing their time listening to things they may or may not have control over, from "coaching" us through. Maybe because of the little time they spend at home, they wish for home to be a sanctuary, free of disgruntled people and sparked emotions, like at work. So if they can find a broad category to throw at it - money, a suggestion to go visit the family, to take a girls trip, an apology - they have convinced themselves that their offers to fix how we feel is the same as understanding.

I gather this might be true for
more than just coaching husbands.

I'm sure there are husbands, and wives, too, who aren't traveling and spending long days in the office, but who are also not comfortable with empathy and who have no desire to connect with their spouses' thoughts if it means going through listening to and validating their emotions first. Even if The Fixer-Upper is able to fix something (temporarily), that connection is superficial and task specific, and the need for shared understanding still lies under the surface.

The most frustrating thing about The Fixer-Upper is that they are often invited as much as they invite themselves. People simply don't realize they desire connection and to be heard more than the situation to be fixed. Because of this human desire to be heard, I can't stress enough how vital it is to learn to keep ourselves in our own shoes while sifting through others' emotions, so we don't become enmeshed in theirs, in order to hear our commonality through thoughts and experiences. It is a skill that should be taught and practiced as a basic social skill and human etiquette, similar to someone saying *bless you* after a sneeze. The ABC models helps people, like Fixer-Uppers, to feel less intimidated by emotions so they don't run away from connection and understanding.

THE CROSSING GUARD

On my childhood street in Bond Hill, there is a mixture of kids who attend the neighborhood elementary public school and the Catholic school, St. Agnes, that sits right across the street. The kids on my street walk to school together as our parents rush to their cars or run to the bus stop to avoid being late for work. If kids aren't already on the porch or walking down the sidewalk, we yell their names as we approach, letting them know we are outside. We take the long route to school, avoiding the darker streets, shaded by dense trees and lined with pitbulls.

As we get closer to school, an elderly man, bundled up in a coat, hat, and a yellow guard vest draped over his shoulders, sits in a folded lawn chair on California Avenue, a canister on the ground next to him. A cigarette hangs from his lips as he gets up from his chair, smiles carefully so that he doesn't lose his smoke, and shouts, "Good morning, boys and girls! Wait until I tell you to go." The man briskly walks toward us, meeting us at the beginning of the street. While walking us across, he hysterically barks at approaching drivers.

"Now, I know you see me here! Y'all better stop."

"Shouldn't be driving that fast anyway."

"It's a school zone, and don't nobody care you are late for work. Should've gotten up earlier."

The old man jumps up and does his job when he sees us approaching. He walks us across the busy street, making sure that we are safe and even prepared.

"Everybody got their books and lunch before I walk you across this street?" The fairly short walk across the street seems much longer; long enough for us to have a morning and afternoon encounter that impacts our day. We joke about how one day our faithful crossing guard will be caught sleeping in the folded lawn chair, not ready for us. But this never happens. He is always watching and waiting, and when we arrive, he meets us where we are.

The Crossing Guard makes it safe to walk through.

One of the first techniques that counselors are taught is active listening. Active listening includes strategies that improve your ability to hear not only what someone says out loud but to hear their feelings and beliefs in the unspoken subtext. Rephrasing, open body language, and literally repeating what someone is saying are a few examples of active listening. The Crossing Guard is not always formally taught these strategies, but he knows how to use them. The Crossing Guard is the ideal expression of empathy that walks through each ABC step of empathy. He acknowledges the fullness of your humanity, acutely aware of the traffic of distractions, losses, and heartaches that are bound to approach your crosswalk, and of your human response to them.

He does not ascribe to the miseducation of empathy—to putting yourself in someone else's shoes so you can try and feel what they are feeling. Instead, The Crossing Guard is comfortable with wide and healthy boundaries, bypassing his feelings in order to validate yours. Because he or she remains an active listener, they are clear and objective with a keen awareness of the distinguishment between your personal crosswalk from theirs. The reflective gear, similar to their ability to listen, tells you it is safe to reflect on what's going on, to bounce off ideas and thoughts, and express how you feel. The Crossing Guard is comfortable with the expression of all kinds of feelings because there is no risk of taking them on. The Crossing Guard is only a reflection. He walks with you, not in place of you.

The Crossing Guard slows down
and halts incoming traffic.

The real essence of empathy lays in the balance between being able to listen without monopolizing the space and guiding a person through with understanding. The Crossing Guard doesn't spend time on critical thinking skills like The Operator, and will not provide you with the same abundance of action steps and resources, leaving you to feel passed off, nor is he anything like The Fixer-Upper. He is patient and values connection in helping, instead of fixing a problem to avoid interaction and connection. Crossing Guards are intentional with helping through the process. They hold up a psycho-emotional stop sign for you and halt incoming negative self-talk, catastrophizing, overgeneralizations, and anything that minimizes your experiences or invalidates your feelings. The Crossing Guard clears space for you in a supportive, safe way.

The Crossing Guard is there to help you slow down enough to challenge your false beliefs, to validate your emotions by making sure they're matched to honest thoughts, without questioning, judging or discouraging you. They walk alongside you, matching your pace in support and solidarity, mindful of your speed in your shoes, looking for opportunities to share understanding in their common thoughts and beliefs.

My best friend became my Crossing Guard during my latter years in college. I met Amber during AAU basketball at seventeen, my junior year in high school. She traveled from the Columbus, Ohio area to play on our Cincinnati team for years, long before I arrived. Being new to the team and new to the sport, she showed me patience, encouragement, and grace, and welcomed me in. We became instant friends and remained friends between our commitments to our rival college basketball teams that were no more than four miles apart. She played at the University of Cincinnati.

Early on, we were both consumed with adjusting to college as scholarship athletes and spent a few hours here and there connecting, but as we finished our junior and senior years, and explored the next steps, we spent more time connecting, listening, challenging each other's thoughts, and sometimes even laughing out loud about our irrational ones. We encouraged one another through good and bad dating decisions, career moves, and life transitions, all the while giving each other permission to feel however we felt. We have shared pure joy and crippling sadness together and rarely have our emotions ever been consumed by each other's. The relationship has been a consistent well of empathy over twenty-five years. A reflection of a shared journey through life's incoming traffic.

Expressing empathy as a Crossing Guard takes time and patience and strategy for listening and understanding. And unfortunately, the miseducation of empathy makes it that much harder. Because of the way we have been taught empathy, we don't even recognize true empathy when it approaches us as a Crossing Guard. Their effectiveness is minimized, if even given the opportunity.

When someone expresses understanding without expressing the same emotion, we deem them as "not really understanding," at times as disloyal, or not "woke" to what's happening to us. We question being understood by The Crossing Guard as they set healthy boundaries and keep their shoes on their own feet. We have been programmed to look for others to be mad right along with us and then calling that validation.

Empathy can't be ruled out because feelings aren't felt within.

Crossing Guards are the epitome expression of empathy, and we are not allowing them to walk us through, because we struggle to recognize them as the reflection of safety, validation, and understanding that they are. Some of us look for weighted blankets and then become uncomfortable when they become too hot. Some of us are left feeling disconnected when "fixed" or "redirected" to resources but can't put our finger on why we still feel so disconnected and deprived. Many of us are frustrated with the cheerleaders in our lives who we honor as positive people that we actually value in our lives. Yet, we are left feeling guilty about not being understood by well-intentioned, optimistic people.

Empathy's Reputation is on the Line

There comes a specific time in our lives when we reflect on the past in order to direct our future; a time when we look back and think about which wrong turns resulted in a longer detour, which relationships helped us find a new path, and about other relationships and circumstances that prolonged our destination. While reflecting, we reimagine our future based on what we learned and experienced. Reflecting on career moves and decisions shapes our idea of our purpose and why we were put on this earth. Reflecting on love and dating relationships impacts our vision for what love and intimacy really mean to us moving forward. I've looked back over connection and the impact of empathy in my life, and I reimagine it being more identifiable, more obtainable and intentional, less confusing and frustrating, more present and more provoking.

Empathy provokes me to be compassionate, accepting, patient, and forgiving, not as an obligation to my faith nor as a sacrifice for my marriage, but because there is a rooted foundation of connection and understanding that lays underneath. Without empathy, I lose out on the opportunity to fully carry out these things activated by empathy. Without empathy, I am distracted and my focus remains on the surface issues rather than the disconnection underneath the surface. In the absence of empathy, I would still be focused on the sacrifices I make as a coach's wife, and Jeff's unwillingness to put himself in my shoes. I'd still be worried and concerned about being associated or affiliated with people who don't dress, act, or think like me. Without true empathy, I'd be fixated on the ignorant comments of intolerance and bigotry by the nice yet uneducated people I sit next to in church.

I'd simply be preoccupied with Band-Aids and ice.

My focus would be on trying to bandage up and ice down the surface manifestations and swelling symptoms of heightened enmeshed emotions, overshadowing connected shared thoughts and the acknowledgement of humanity's imperfections laying under the inflammation. Unfortunately, empathy has always been taught as Band-Aids and ice. A semi-effective way to temporarily stop the swelling and contain the bleeding.

Empathy is surgery, cutting through the flesh toward disjointedness.

My parent's performed surgery on me. They dissected my thoughts and stitched them with theirs, sifting through the specifics of their stories, careful not to tip the scale of comparison by emphasizing the drastic differences in their childhood hardships. They understood that empathy had to be taught to me and didn't get upset when it didn't just come naturally. Growing up as a little girl, I watched my parents model this with each other and with my childhood friend, Claudine, distinguishing themselves from neighbors who showed her pity instead. And yet, I couldn't definitively name what I was being taught. This empathy wasn't the metaphor of shoes learned in school and it wasn't the golden rule I was taught in church. It was a specific practice with investigative skills. A practice of skills that later had me questioning my ability to connect with girls in college, where most of them spent more time being surrogates for other's feelings, rather than a bridge of shared experiences and thoughts.

College, and the transition from being a high school athlete to a Division 1 basketball player, is when I needed empathy the most. My feelings were so overwhelming that the last thing I wanted to do was invite a surrogate to bear my feelings, too. I intentionally looked for this connection through my teammates, boyfriends, roommates, friends, and later on my sorority sisters. And I did find glimpses of the various characters of empathy. My sophomore boyfriend was a Cheerleader who just wanted to stay positive and cheer me through the difficult times when I felt like I didn't belong and wasn't good enough. He wanted no part of my sadness or my dwindling self-esteem that was rooted in the belief that I was not enough. I had professors and advisors who were Fixer-Uppers, who didn't spend much time listening for understanding and just offered avenues for me to continue my studies on campus without having to play a game I had just fallen in love with four years before. I had coaches who were Operators, who were more concerned with my performance on the basketball court and outsourcing any understanding of me beyond that. But thankfully, in my final two years, I had some Crossing Guards, and Blankets who were thin enough to become Crossing Guards. I had friends I met in graduate school, sorority sisters, and counseling mentors who listened and recognized my need for their emotional boundaries. They got to know me well enough to be cautious about not wearing my shoes. Their empathy provoked sisterhood and reflected a spirit of shared empowerment, resilience, and my re-introduction to vulnerability.

Empathy provokes vulnerability by reducing the risks associated with it.

Vulnerability is putting ourselves out there, being emotionally exposed and taking a risk in expressing our truth, This can lead to cathartic self-discovery, healing, freedom, and connection through the imperfections of our shared humanity. Vulnerability doesn't lead to these things without the practice of empathy. We need to acknowledge that humanity itself is vulnerable. We need to bypass our own feelings that typically distract, overwhelm, or block someone else from being vulnerable enough to express theirs in the midst of yours, and we need to connect our shared thoughts to cultivate an atmosphere of oneness and non-judgement that reduces the risks, fears, and uncertainty that comes with someone being vulnerable.

Empathy provokes courage for others to be vulnerable.

As I look back on the role empathy played in my marriage, I'm optimistic about how to provoke more love, more patience, and more forgiveness in it now and in the future through the practice of empathy toward my husband. No longer confusing empathy and understanding with mutual sacrificial obligations, I am confident in expressing what I really need to feel understood - validation and permission to feel how I feel, and expressed connection of thought and experiences in lieu of him suffering along with me. And I realize I am a better wife, and our marriage is a better union when I reciprocate this for Jeff, and even for myself. Being empathetic toward myself provokes the same characteristics - self-love, self-acceptance, and forgiveness of myself - which, in turn, makes me a healthier partner.

Empathy provokes you to overcome your insecurities.

It is a common and accepted principle that you should take care of yourself in order to better take care of others. The flight attendant reminds us every time we get on a plane that in the case of an emergency, you are to put on your oxygen mask before putting masks on the children in your care.

You cannot pour from an empty cup.

The insecurities I developed on Xavier's campus about making lifelong friends and playing basketball are insecurities that I have to overcome even today. The underlying themes of those insecurities of "not being good enough to play" and "not being understood enough to fit in" linger around in my marriage, manifest in my career, and rear its ugly head in my parenting. I have to constantly implement the ABCs with myself. A. Acknowledge that I'm not superhuman and will make mistakes. B. I have to constantly bypass my reactive, spontaneous feelings and investigate my thoughts behind them. And then I have to place myself in the safe company of God, and/or people with shared thoughts and beliefs, so I feel connected to inspiration and motivation and hope to overcome. God even connects me to my own past thoughts and experiences that walked me through vulnerability and adversity. (God's love is the practice of empathy.) Those moments of empathy that I expressed to myself and that were shared with me during the onset of Kayla's diagnosis of alopecia empowers me to face the same insecurities of not being good enough, not being a good enough mom, head-on. In the midst of the sympathy that surrounded me, empathy prevailed in inspiring me to be a resilient, patient, loving mommy.

We have flaunted the term *empathy* around as the solution to almost every human social problem, and yet we continue to perpetuate the miseducation of empathy by likening it to other terms, minimizing the execution of it, and not fully comprehending its impactfulness. We need to fully understand the devastation of sympathy, the influence it may have on people's lives, and how it should never be confused with empathy. To understand empathy, we must also understand the power of comparison to cancel out the opportunity for empathetic relationships, and the fear of association or affiliation abolishing any chance of connected understanding. We need to be aware of the imposters and characters that fall short in representing this seven-letter, three-syllable word that we place so much trust in. If we don't know that we are acting as imposters and/or deficient characters of empathy in an attempt to show understanding with the people we love, then we won't ever come to the revelation of why people are not responding to our efforts of understanding.

For my life, the miseducation of empathy falls short in helping uncover what's beneath feelings of self-doubt and of inadequacy, especially when they're dressed in pride, leaving me to fend for myself and afraid to solicit support. It doesn't cultivate a climate of vulnerability and safety that relieves my fears of judgement and my fear that others will adopt my already overwhelming feelings. It doesn't teach my children specifically how to connect with their peers beyond a notion that is inherited. The miseducation of empathy may have connected me with other mothers with guilt, but it doesn't walk me past comparison, around sympathy, and towards healing and supportive understanding, like true empathy does.

The miseducation of empathy is exhausting.

The miseducation of education is why we are in this ongoing, never-ending conversation about the horrible condition of humanity and about our frustration with the lack of empathy in our country. Empathy has never really lived up to its reputation! It sits in training manuals as a sentiment to consider or ideal to follow. It headlines news articles and magazines as a theory we should all adopt. It scrolls down social media feeds as philosophical quotes and hypothetical questions. "What if our country was a more empathetic one?"

But what if empathy really lived up to its reputation?

When it does, the step by step process to practicing empathy will be the introduction to premarital counseling, the foundation of social skills curriculums, and lessons in student-teaching. When empathy lives up to its reputation, team building, leadership conferences, and church ministry retreats will lecture about the barriers of empathy, and teach on the characters of empathy expressed. When empathy really lives up to its true meaning, diversity and mediation trainings will begin with the ABCs of empathy that set the stage for listening and understanding of differences. Uncomfortable conversations will have a chance to provoke growth and connection when empathy actually lives up to its reputation, and is not reduced to an imagination of feelings.

When empathy really lives up to its reputation, our children will know empathy - not know *of* empathy. They will know specifically how to practice it for themselves and others, rather than reference a Nike slogan or a metaphor about shoes. Our children will see us model the skills, and not infer that it is innate and should just come naturally for them. Kayla will embody empathy so that as she grows older as a beautiful bald woman, she practices empathy with herself! There is too much at stake!

Self-esteem
Confidence

Connection

Community

Unity

True empathy, with a drawn-up game plan and scouting report, provides a space of exploration and discovery where we can excavate who we are and who we are becoming based on the underlying beliefs and motives that initiate how we feel and what we do. It examines our relationships and connections honestly and without interference or sabotaging our temporal emotions. Friendships are rescued by the forgiveness and patience provoked by empathy that understands past shared sentiments.

For twenty-plus years, I have been on this journey of weaving theories about what I have learned in my counseling practice, my religious beliefs, and what I've learned through life's peaks and valleys, and the relationships that accompanied them - weaving together theories of human behavior, spiritual discernment, and my real life in order to define what is required for meaningful understanding and connection with people. People I don't like, and people who don't like me. People who are different from me, and who grew up differently than me. People who present as though they are smarter than me, and those who are. People who share different religious beliefs, and those who share the same but carry out those beliefs completely different than I do. And what I've discovered is that true empathy, regardless of the people or the arena it's played in, once relearned, will live up to its reputation.

ABOUT THE AUTHOR

Jonelle Massey

www.jonellemassey.com

Jonelle Massey knows that successful people are typically exposed to diverse experiences, challenges, and people. This is her twentieth year as an educator and nationally certified licensed mental health therapist, having recieved her master's degree from Xavier University in Cincinnati, Ohio. Jonelle's diverse service in education as a school counselor and therapist includes both public and private, primary and secondary educational settings, as well as psychiatric hospital care and private practice.

Married to a Division I college basketball coach, Jonelle adjusts well to relocation and makes an immediate impact with each professional move. As a former Division I athletic scholarship recipient with Xavier University's women's basketball program, Jonelle shares her passion for teaching effective teamwork, work ethic, connection, and resilience through volunteer coaching at local high schools and consulting with university athletic teams.

While playing collegiate basketball, she received all academic honors all four years and Defensive Player of the Year award her senior year. Her strength in leadership is also evident in her professional development lectures as a school counselor and crisis counselor, community service involvement, and entrepreneur successes in the greater Toledo area.

Jonelle volunteers as an advisor for two chapters of the Young Women of Excellence student leadership group, a small business mentor, board member and advocate for the National Alopecia Areata Foundation, STEMinist with the Imagination Station, and founding member and board liaison of HerHub, a Toledo organization that connects women, resources, businesses, and organizations through an online hub.

A native of Cincinnati, Ohio, Jonelle resides in Toledo, Ohio with her husband, Jeff ("Coach Mass") and two daughters, Aubrey and Kayla.

CPSIA information can be obtained
at www.ICGtesting.com
Printed in the USA
FSHW010024250321
79778FS